Shirley King

Pampille's Table

Pampille's Table

Recipes and Writings
from the French Countryside

SHIRLEY KING

Faber & Faber
Boston · London

Library of Congress Cataloging-in-Publication Data

King, Shirley.
 Pampille's table : recipes and writings from the French
countryside : from Marthe Daudet's Les bons plats de France /
translated and adapted by Shirley King.
  p. cm.
 ISBN 0-571-19889-9 (hc)
 1. Cookery, French. I. Daudet, Marthe, 1878–1960.
Bons plats de France. English. II. Title.
TX719.K563 1996
641.5944–dc20   95-44044
                                                      CIP

Photograph on p. 3
courtesy of Dennis Brack/Black Star

"Truffles in Perigord" p. 43, "Franche Comté" p. 149,
"Carcassone" p. 222, "Auvergne," p. 187, and "Les Gorges de Tarn" p. 199
courtesy of the French Government Tourist Office, New York City

"Gathering Seaweed" p. 123
courtesy of Robert Burton, *The Seashore and its Wildlife*

"Geese in Wantenzenau, near Strasbourg" p. 159
courtesy of Fernand Nathan

"Lorraine" p. 166
courtesy of Bernard Hermann and Abrams Publishing

"Alphonse Daudet's Windmill, Fontveille" p. 207
courtesy of Proctor Jones Publishing Co.

Photos on pp. 7, 135, 180, and 233 by Shirley King.

Jacket design by David Shultz
Jacket photograph of Marthe Daudet, known as Pampille,
used with permission of Mme François Daudet.
Printed in the United States of America

Dedication

In Memoriam

I wish I had known Pampille.
I feel we would have enjoyed each other in the kitchen.

While researching my book *Dining with Marcel Proust* (Thames and Hudson, 1979), I found these references to Pampille, which led me to her book.

"She knows as well as you do that Gallardonette is an old *poison*," went on Mme de Guermantes, whose vocabulary . . . was as richly flavored as those dishes which it is possible to come across in the delicious books of Pampille which have in real life become so rare, dishes in which the jellies, the butter, the sauces, the *quenelles* are all genuine and unalloyed, in which even the salt is brought specially from the salt-marshes of Brittany. . . . (Book II, page 521);

M Verdurin . . . I will go further: in the interest of his own reputation he died at the right moment, *à point*, as the lobsters, grilled according to Pampille's incomparable recipe, are going to be . . . (Book II, page 931);

And if, seizing this point of departure, I led Mme de Guermantes on to talk about the Rohans (with whom her own family had frequently intermarried), her conversation would become impregnated with a hint of the wistful charm of the Breton "pardons" and (as that true poet Pampille would say) with the pungent flavor of buckwheat crepes cooked over a gorse fire. . . . (Book III, page 29).

Remembrance of Things Past, by Marcel Proust,
translated by C. K. Scott Moncrieff, Terence Kilmartin, and
Andreas Mayor, Chatto & Windus, 1981.

Contents

Foreword

I have translated this book because of its intrinsic value to me—to all of us. It is a gastronomic and literary treat. It is a recipe book that is also a travelogue. It is an intriguing mix of charming writing and wonderful, authentic recipes from the different regions of France. It is rare to find such a rich, personal cookbook.

Pampille reveals the regions of France with poetic insights that will make you dream or want to go there. You can see the landscape, hear the birds sing, experience the weather, smell and taste the food. In contrast, her writing can be definitely vitriolic, but it always has an underlying humor, as seen in her essay on The Awful Dinner, which is so much fun to read. The recipes are unadulterated by fashion and style. Here are many beautifully written classics of French cuisine, but the majority of recipes are unusual specialties from twenty regions of France. Typically French, with subtle colors and clean tastes, the regional recipes are a joy to make and eat; they so thoroughly evoke the area and the time. Even the desserts are not too sweet! These recipes, which Pampille acknowledges were gathered from friends, relatives, and gourmands from all over France, are for uncomplicated, homey dishes that probably had not been written down before. Her lucid, unfussy recipes coax us to prepare the lovely food.

Many of these regional specialties have made their way into my repertory—specialties such as *Bouchées Pauillacaises* (Stuffed Potato Balls), Grape Harvester's Turkey Wings, Mussels with Spinach, Eggplant *Provençale*, Grilled Stuffed Sardines, *Garbure*

(Cabbage Soup), Game Surprises from Périgueux (Quail in Parchment Paper Packages), Veal Terrine Armenonville (Rillettes of Veal), the best Onion Soup I have ever eaten, a Macaroni *Timbale*, seafood dishes from Normandy and Brittany, a chocolate cake called *Le Beau Ténébreux* (a stunning savoy cake, filled with *crème fraîche*, glazed with chocolate), an Amaretti (macaroon) Soufflé, and *Bourdelots* (pastry-covered pears or apples).

When you read this jewel of a book, it becomes obvious that Pampille was a fascinating character who lived in a fascinating time. She constantly imparts her enthusiasm for food, as if she wanted to encourage people to enjoy cooking and eating again after the horrible shortages of the First World War. These recipes can be made just as successfully today.

On the whole, the dishes are made with readily available ingredients. A few recipes are difficult to adhere to, but only a few. After all, seventy-five years ago such animals as hares were common. There are only seven recipes that use truffles — a nice change from other books of that era! And, surprisingly, her recipes do not rely heavily on cream or eggs.

I have adapted her recipes so they work for us today. I have tried to keep out of Pampille's way, using her original tone and syntax as much as possible in the translation. The recipes are now a collaboration, for I have made them all — roast hare and acacia blossom *beignets* excepted! Large rabbits can be used instead of hares and zucchini blossoms can be used if you can't find acacia blossoms. In the United States we have to be happy with duck livers instead of goose, which is no great shame.

Acknowledgments

To Kate Lovelady who helped in editing, Tamara Holt for help on the research and testing recipes, and Frances Cleary who also tested recipes, many thanks. To my friend Alex Karmel who translated some of the more difficult and convoluted passages with finesse, thanks. Ellen Sowchek did some in-depth translations of some words and sentences, for which I am most grateful. Peter Pullman pulled me out of some grammatical jams. Many thanks to Jack Ubaldi for guiding me to American equivalent cuts of meat. My thanks to my ever-industrious agent, Judith Weber, who understands my passion for this book; and to my editor Valerie Cimino, who is so enthusiastic about this small but astonishing book. My sincere thanks to Mme François Daudet for permission to translate and use her photograph of Pampille—Marthe Daudet.

Equipment Used in an
Early Twentieth-Century French Kitchen

Although there were gas stoves as early as 1850, Pampille's warnings on not letting the fire go out suggest that she used a stove fueled by wood, coal, or charcoal. (Vine shoots could also be used as fuel to add a special flavor.) This type of stove had multiple purposes. The chimney from the stove helped to heat the house and to warm water. There were several ovens, each at a different temperature according to their proximity to the main source of heat. The top was polished iron and also of varying temperatures — thus Pampille's phrase, "brown on the corner of the stove," meant away from the main heat. These stoves were much like the English AGA stoves that are used today.

Often a stove of that period had a built-in rotisserie on the side, and on top, a built-in *bain-marie*, a space filled with heated water to keep containers of food warm.

As well as using the home stove, it was the custom to take slow-cooking dishes to the baker's to take advantage of the dwindling heat of the oven after he had baked the bread for the day.

Recommended Pots and Pans for this Book

For the dishes in this book, apart from the usual kitchen equipment I recommend that you have an 8- to 10-quart capacity stockpot, also called a *pot-au-feu* or *marmite*; a heavy, deep casserole with a lid; a 12-inch frying pan; a 12-inch shallow earthenware casserole; an 8-cup soufflé dish or eight to twelve ½-cup ramekins, a food mill, a food processor, and a blender. If you want to make the Steamed Truffled Bresse Hen you will need a 16-quart capacity stockpot. A stainless steel *rondeau* (a heavy round pot about 15 inches in diameter and 6 to 7 inches deep with a lid) is also useful.

Pampille's Table

The Awful Dinner

The classic awful dinner is usually held in a dining room painted too brilliantly white and furnished with ugly, pretentious, awkward, and misshapen furniture in which it is impossible to be comfortable.

The table is richly decorated by the florist with orchids. The silver cutlery sparkles, the crystal glasses shine, the wine carafes glow, and the lights blaze. The tablecloth is edged here and there with real lace. But in spite of all this luxury, tremble! For our hostess has packed in eighteen guests at the table. The best dinners happen when eight to ten good friends gather together. With higher numbers, the guests can't bond and there is no real

opportunity for interesting conversation. The guests sit with
their noses in their plates and talk only to their immediate
neighbors. If your dinner partner is a bore, you begin to feel as
if you are slowly dying.

I know the hostess: she is one of those who attach more importance to the pleasures of the eye than to the pleasures of the
palate. She orders the dinner, writes out the menus, telephones
the florist and the ice-cream shop, and thinks her work is done.
Then she goes out visiting all day long and returns home just in
time to dress for dinner. What cheek and negligence! . . .

So I worry from the start of the dinner. I know that the soup
was ladled into the soup bowls far in advance, so that it will in-
evitably arrive tepid, not hot. It vaguely resembles a *consommé
à la reine* [a clear broth] in which three small peas and some
cubes of egg swim. The serving in the hollow of the soup plate
is so small that one might as well not have any at all.

For those who do not yet know, learn now that *soup must be
served hot.* We eat soup at the beginning of the meal to dilate
our stomachs. Its aroma should make us feel hungry. It lines
our stomachs like a soft carpet so we can eat spicy foods without danger, but this doesn't mean it has to be as thick and heavy
as dog food.

Why isn't the soup served boiling hot from a soup tureen, so
that guests can take as much as they want?

After the soup, here come the *lucullus bouchées* [puff pastry
cases]. What do we find inside them? Alas, the same ingredients as in all *bouchées* with this name: little bits of cat's brain,
three mushrooms, and a *quenelle* [forcemeat] pale as a drowned
man's finger. All of this stuck together with a gluey white sauce
or maybe a brown, viscous liquid called *financière.*

And now what is this fishy smell? They are bringing in the
brill, and there is a strong smell of iodine. As it is passed cere-
moniously around, everyone takes as little as possible. It is certainly large enough, in fact it is magnificent, except that you

can see its bones protruding along its back, as if it had shed its corset. It has traveled extensively—it has been in the heat, it has had to wait in railroad stations. The fishmonger tried to revive it, in vain, by placing it on ice. Imagine the nasty surprise the hostess will get when she sees the bill—and she thought she was buying a fresh fish!

Ris de veau [calf sweetbreads] follows our brill, which was not a great success. Let's bet that the sweetbreads have not been picked clean. *Ris de veau* is a homey dish that needs a lot of attention. It is excellent when coated with a wonderful meat glaze and served on a bed of spinach or chicory. But it is a banal dish to serve at a grand dinner, especially when the cook is too busy to take the time to prepare the sweetbreads properly.

A fillet of beef, nearly burned to ashes and no longer having a drop of blood between its fibers, makes its appearance. It is surrounded with stuffed mushrooms and tasteless tomatoes—in the bargain it has arrived half cold. Of course it is no surprise to see peas served straight out of the jar without seasoning. Ah! if I could only get hold of the cook!

On to the *pâté de foie gras* [goose liver pâté] and our salvation. We are hungry now, but it is just a light mousse. It doesn't have the consistency of a *pâté en croute* [pâté in pastry] that is pink and soft and melts in your mouth. Instead, the liver has been whipped up with cream, and it has been overworked. Each mouthful is a phantom, leaving no more taste in the mouth than a little snow.

We are served a kirsch ice cream to finish. Unfortunately, desserts made with liquor are the ones I hate the most.

We are revived with *petits fours* and some fruit, which I have to admit is marvelous. The selection of fruits served is the signature of an expensive dinner—but this does not necessarily mean the dinner was good.

The wines, though famous, are rarely passed. The *maître d'hôtel* [the steward], with an air of mystery, confides their age to us, probably to reassure us. Water is featured generously, and there are all sorts: Evian, Châteline, Vichy, and so on. The hostess is proud of her selection, but the only really good water, water from the tap, is not featured on this table.

Returning home after such a bad dinner, our only wish is to eat some bread and cheese and munch on an apple. You can't imagine how wonderful an apple tastes after midnight.

Seasonal Fruits and Vegetables

Judging the season by the little bit of sky seen above the roofs between the twirling weather vanes and chimneys, but misled by the premature blossoming of the far-too-intelligent trees of Paris, a Parisian can nevertheless always tell with great precision the month and the date by the appearance of a succession of fruits and vegetables.

When the mandarins are no longer juicy and dry up in their skins like little mummies, and when oranges no longer have fresh, taut skins like bright new tennis balls, we start to brighten up, for it is the end of the black days. Doubtless the wind will still blow under the doors and send up gusts of dust in the dry streets, but this is not the same wind, for this wind chases away the wintry sky, and we catch a glimpse of a little corner of warm, tender blue sky and start to laugh ourselves into spring.

During the weeks between, fruits are rare. Bananas, sold from little carts, are the only fruits found in abundance. North and South America divert their full ocean liners into our streets. The last pears have hearts of ice, or their flesh has become gritty. The last apples have lost their scent, so you no longer think you are eating an invisible rose when you bite into their white sweet flesh. Calvilles are the best; Reinettes are wrinkled like little old ladies; Canadian apples smell of old cardboard. All that are left are the Api apples that can enhance a compote. They may not be extraordinary, but their shiny red faces lying in green moss are always a happy sight.

Les quatres mendiants [the four orders of mendicant friars: Augustin, Carmelite, Dominican, and Franciscan] appear to be dispersed to the four cardinal points. [*Les quatres mendiants* is a dessert consisting of four kinds of dried fruits—almonds, figs, hazelnuts, and raisins.] The good simple prune has turned into sugar and is no longer edible.

From the end of February, you notice in the greengrocer's shop windows—which begin to resemble the windows of jewelry shops—strawberries lying on beds of cotton in little wooden boxes. They are beautiful, and huge, but still a little pale. They are a marvel, but they are never good to eat so early. Leave them for the American millionaires who would be hard put to spend their money if they weren't able to pay a hundred thousand francs for a tasteless strawberry—we will wait a bit longer before feasting on strawberries. Soon the good ones will appear, mostly large ones from market gardens; entire long trainloads of them will cross Paris, leaving in their wake the odor of fruit instead of smoke. Next come the wild strawberries, tiny strawberries in small baskets, so delicate they must have been picked by elves. These berries taste of leaves and the dawn; eat them with closed eyes and be instantly transported to the edge of a forest.

Large asparagus make their appearance at the same time as the strawberries. Carefully tied together in large and small bunches, these are important creatures. They know their value and are highly admired by gourmands. Beside them is a hamper, covered or not, filled with shelled green peas, prompting the cry from the merchants, "*C'est la tendresse, la verduresse!...*" [Tender and green!]. Baby haricot beans in tiny baskets, so young they have not had time to give birth, are also exhibited for our admiration.

A little later on, maybe fifteen days later, the cherries in their turn, treated like princesses, are placed in padded boxes. They are the first cherries and are not up to much. You have to wait until the month of May for them to swell up with juice and take on the taste of the sun. But we must not anticipate.

At the end of March and in the first days of April come the morels. Small morels are the best. The merchants place them carefully in creaking wicker baskets, and connoisseurs fight over them. They are right to do so, for the morel is an exquisite mushroom, friend to veal and chicken. But alas, morels don't last long! Hardly fifteen days to three weeks after their appearance come the giant morels, which are not nearly so good. Yet they also disappear quickly.

May brings us almonds. The first are deceptive; often in place of an almond there is only a little sugared jelly under the yellow pulp. But the days pass, the almond hardens, and soon our teeth are biting into them, the pleasure as much in the noise as in the taste.

From then on, fruits and vegetables are abundant. There are tons of strawberries: they get crushed in their baskets and spoil in the shop window—even the flies don't want them. There are so many asparagus that they overflow their little carts and are not worth more than a bunch of violets. There are so many cherries that they fall down from their pyramids and get sticky and covered with dust before you can buy them.

A little surprise in the month of June happens when the gooseberries and the raspberries arrive.

Summer abounds with a great variety of fruits. We have juicy apricots, exquisite peaches, sweet plums, figs, melons, and, at the end of the season, pears, apples, and beautiful black and white grapes that we have to put up with patiently until the month of January.

One fruit ripens in November: it is the medlar. It is often misunderstood, though it does the best it can. It is best to make preserves with them—which resembles a jam of dead leaves, and evokes the loneliness of shepherds. The best way to savor it is to feel a little sad and eat it near a fire with a teaspoon, being careful not to break your teeth on the pits.

I

National Dishes

Pot-au-Feu — *A Beef and Turkey or Chicken Giblet Soup*
Boiled Beef
Onion Soup
Cabbage Soup
Leek and Potato Soup
Poule au Pot — *Chicken Soup*
Consommé de Sorcier — *Sorcerer's Consommé*

Boeuf à la Mode — *Braised Beef*
Spoon-Tender Beef
Chicken Fricassee with Pearl Onions

RAGOUTS — STEWS
Lamb and Bean Ragout
Navarin — *A Lamb Stew*

Stuffed Cabbage

GAME
Quail Risotto
Civet de Lièvre — *Hare Ragout*
Rabbit, Hunter-Style
Pheasant à la Sainte-Alliance,
from La Physiologie du Goût *by Brillat-Savarin*

Simple Omelet
Potato Salad

Royal Pudding à la Dutrait-Crozen

Dear reader of this small book, do not expect new or complicated recipes, or menus for grand dinners with elaborate set pieces. I am incapable of giving them; books by wise men such as Chef Durand or Brillat-Savarin can enlighten you on such subjects. My ambition is not so grand—I don't pretend to have invented anything new—I want only to try and group together some of the best traditional recipes of French cooking and to present the most characteristic recipes from each region. If I succeed with this little mosaic, which is unfortunately incomplete, it is due to all my friends, relatives, and the many gourmands that I have encountered in my life. I can't list all their names—there are too many of them—but I thank them very much for so generously giving me their secrets.

Before divulging these secrets, I should add that a good recipe does not guarantee a perfect dish. There is a certain something called *la tour de main*—a special touch—that contributes to at least half the success of any dish. In general, fat cooks are endowed with this special touch more than thin cooks. But even this special touch is not enough unless a little love is also an ingredient. People who are grim faced and sulky in the kitchen, who swear that this is the worst of all professions, obviously will not produce anything worthwhile. Those who cook at full speed and say, "that will have to do," are just plain sabotaging the whole process. The truth is that cooking is not a profession—it is a calling. A calling that brings a real and immediate joy.

Four Great Soups

Now let's talk about the four most important national soups of France. They come from the north and south, the east and west, and they are the basic food of the country folk. You probably know them already and can guess their names: *Pot-au-Feu,* Onion Soup, Cabbage Soup, and Leek and Potato Soup.

These four poetic soups are worth careful study.

Pot-au-Feu—
A Beef and Turkey or Chicken Giblet Soup

You have to be at least 30 years old to enjoy *Pot-au-Feu*. Before reaching this prophetic age, you cannot appreciate good things. You may consider the *pot-au-feu* commonplace, and as you do with its old pal, boiled beef, scorn it. This is a terrible mistake, but it is rectified as the years pass by. There is nothing better than a well made *pot-au-feu* when cooks deign to give it all their attention and care.

It is laughable that doctors would have us think that the broth contains dangerous toxins, because we know that a good, hot, concentrated broth, properly salted, has never harmed anyone. On the contrary, it is a wonderful comfort and the best remedy for fatigue and lassitude.

Here is a straightforward recipe for making an excellent soup, taken from a cook who spent 30 years with the same family and never took a course in modern cookery.

4	quarts cold water
4	large carrots
3	white turnips
1	bunch leeks, trimmed of root ends and tough green leaves, cut lengthwise and rinsed
3	pounds beef shank
1	set of turkey or chicken giblets—feet, neck, wings, and gizzard—[or 2 chicken drumsticks]
3	ounces calf's liver
6	2-inch-long pieces of marrow bone
3	tablespoons coarse salt
1	medium tomato
2	onions, one stuck with a clove

Use a *pot-au-feu*—a large 8- to 10-quart pot. Treat this pot like a friend, taking great care of it and using it *solely* for making broths, soups, and stocks.

Fill the pot to one-third with cold water—about 4 quarts.

Peel your vegetables carefully. Cut the carrots and turnips into 3 or 4 pieces each if they are large. Tie the leeks together with string so they will not separate while cooking.

Place your meat and giblets in the pot; add the calf's liver, marrow bones, and coarse salt. Bring to a boil over moderate heat. Skim once before it comes to a boil.

When it is boiling, add all your vegetables but reserve one onion — the one without the clove. Add the onion skins as long as they are clean, because they add color to the stock.

Lower the heat so that the water continues to simmer evenly and slowly, *without interruption,* for 4 to 6 hours. After 4 hours you will have a decently flavored stock; after 6 hours it is more flavorful and colorful.

After 2 hours, when the *pot-au-feu* is cooking nicely, cut the second onion in half crosswise and brown both halves, cut side down, in a frying pan with a teaspoon of oil. Add it to the stock.

Note: One can substitute a handful of pea pods that have been dried out in the oven for the browned onion. The pea pods come in little bundles tied with string from certain regions in the center of France, such as Touraine. The pea pods color the stock and give it an excellent taste.

Artificial colors are detestable and *one must not use them.*

Remove the fat with a soup ladle. When ready to serve the soup, taste it and add salt and pepper as needed. Place very thin slices of toasted bread in a soup tureen. Place a strainer over the tureen; bring the soup to a boil and strain it into the tureen. When it is full, serve the soup, with the vegetables on a separate platter. The vegetables are usually overcooked — they have given their all to the stock. Serve freshly cooked vegetables in the soup. If the soup has been prepared exactly as I have written, with fresh meat and fresh vegetables and a browned onion added to color it, it should be golden, aromatic, clear, and delicious. But it takes so little to spoil it! Old meat, one bad giblet, an interruption in the simmering, not using the right proportions, too few carrots, and the stock will be pale, insipid, even sad.

Cooks have a tendency to make too much at a time. It is best to take my advice and make enough for one meal and if there is any left over, save it for the next day to make a risotto (page 32) or a rich macaroni (page 92). Freeze any remaining stock.

Serves 8.

Boiled Beef— ### *Referring to the Beef Cooked in the* Pot-au-Feu

Now let's talk about boiled beef. The meat, of course, loses flavor after lengthy cooking and becomes fibrous and dry. The shank makes the best broth, and in my opinion it is the best cut of beef to use because it stays moist, whereas breast meat or eye rounds become stringy without exception.

The shank—butchers call it the *bas morceau*—is a real treat for connoisseurs. One can serve it in many ways.

One of the best ways that I know, when tomatoes are in season, is to surround the cooked meat with halved and seeded tomatoes. Marinate them for at least an hour beforehand in a rich vinaigrette. Boiled potatoes complete the garnish.

The beef is also excellent served with fresh noodles and a thick tomato sauce.

Some people do not serve the vegetables with the *pot-au-feu,* but instead place them around the meat.

An accompaniment that is very good in winter is a well-cooked and drained savoy cabbage, served with some slices of slab bacon. Cook the cabbage *separately* for 10 minutes in boiling salted water and not in the broth, because it will spoil the taste of the broth.

Garnishes

A lettuce salad dressed with some mayonnaise and hard-cooked eggs cut in quarters will go well with this dish.

Finally, there are gourmands who are sick and tired of all the different accompaniments, who prefer their boiled beef simply as it comes: with coarse salt. But they should obtain this salt from the salt-marsh districts such as Piriac, at Mme Béchet's grocery shop in Piriac, Loire-Inférieure. They say that this salt is like no other, and that each grain contains a tiny piece of the landscape.

Onion Soup

[This is the best onion soup I have ever eaten. The addition of a mixture of pink, black, white, and green peppercorns and Jamaican allspice ground over the bread makes all the difference. This mixture, very flavorful and aromatic, is sold under different brand names such as the name Pepper Mélange by Select Origins, obtainable in specialty stores (see Sources, page 265). You can assemble your own mixture easily. *Quatre épices* (see Glossary, page 263), is another aromatic mixture of black pepper, nutmeg, cinnamon, and ground cloves that can be used.]

     2   ounces (½ stick) unsalted butter
    2¼   pounds onions, thinly sliced
     5   cups beef and chicken stock, *Poule-au-Pot* recipe,
         (page 21) [or 1½ chicken bouillon cubes and 1 beef
         cube dissolved in 5 cups water] or see Note below
         Salt to taste
     4   tablespoons *crème fraîche* (see Glossary, page 260)
    16   slices bread, cut in 3-inch squares or rounds
         Freshly ground black pepper, or see note above
     ½   pound Parmesan or Gruyère cheese, grated

Melt the butter in a large heavy saucepan over moderate to high heat. Add the sliced onions and brown them well. Browning the onions takes up to ¾ hour—be patient and stir occasionally to prevent them from burning.

Add the stock little by little, stirring all the time with a wooden spoon.

Add a little salt and boil for ¼ hour.

Add the *crème fraîche*.

Preheat the oven to 425 degrees. Line a round earthenware casserole with thin slices of stale or toasted bread, sprinkled heavily with black pepper, then a layer of Parmesan or Gruyère cheese (Parmesan is better), then another layer of peppered bread and grated cheese.

Pour the soup on top and bake for 15 minutes, until bubbling hot and golden brown!

Note: In case you do not have a rich stock on hand, a stock made with fresh shelled white haricot beans, broad beans, or lentils, and so on, will give good flavor to the soup. [This stock will appeal to vegetarians.] Certain people add plain ordinary boiling water and a spoonful of flour. But I confess that I prefer onion soup made without flour.

Serves 8.

Cabbage Soup

In order to make a true cabbage soup, you must own a *marmite*—a large 8- to 10-quart pot. The lamb breast, if previously sprinkled with salt and pepper and well browned on the grill, is wonderful to eat after the soup. You can serve it on a vegetable puree or simply with a *Rémoulade* Sauce, see page 56. This soup is excellent reheated.

3   quarts cold water
1   pound pork belly or salt pork, soaked for a few hours
    in several changes of cold water or a lamb bone or
    1 pound lamb breast (previously grilled, broiled,
    sautéed, or roasted until browned)
3   large carrots, peeled and sliced
2   onions, one of them stuck with a clove
2   turnips, peeled and cubed
⅔   cup dried white beans
4   medium-size red bliss potatoes, peeled and cubed
1   pound fava beans, shelled
½   pound peas, shelled
1   savoy cabbage, cored and cut in 8 wedges
    Salt and freshly ground pepper
1   baguette, sliced

Place the water and pork belly or lamb in the *marmite*. Bring to
a boil; skim. Add the carrots, onions, turnips, and beans. Simmer for a total of 1¼ hours.

Add the potatoes in the last 20 minutes, and the fava beans,
peas, and cabbage in the last 10 minutes. Add salt and
pepper—but not too much salt if you are using salt pork!

Ladle the soup into bowls, over slices of bread.

Serves 8.

Leek and Potato Soup

The authentic leek and potato soup has bread soaked in it and must be thick.

2 quarts cold water
1 bunch leeks, trimmed of root ends and tough green
   leaves, cut lengthwise, rinsed and chopped
4 medium-size potatoes, peeled and cubed
   Salt
   Freshly ground black pepper
8 slices stale bread from a French baguette
4 tablespoons *crème fraîche* (see Glossary, page 260)
2 tablespoons unsalted butter

Bring the water to a boil in a stockpot.

Throw the leeks and potatoes into the boiling water. Add salt and pepper.

Simmer for 30 minutes.

Place the sliced bread in the bottom of the soup tureen. Stir the *crème fraîche* and butter into the soup, blending well.

Pour your soup into the tureen *without straining it.* Alternatively, you can put the soup through a food mill.

Serves 8.

Poule-au-Pot — *Chicken Soup*

When you want to make this chicken soup, proceed exactly as in the recipe for *Pot-au-Feu* (see page 14), except of course substitute chicken for the beef shank.

1 5-pound hen or boiling fowl or a roasting chicken

Cook a boiling hen or fowl for 3 to 4 hours or a roasting chicken for 1½ hours. Boiled chicken served with a good béarnaise sauce (see page 51) is a delight—it is one of those simple dishes you will never tire of.

Serves 8 to 10.

Consommé de Sorcier—*Sorcerer's Consommé*
(Dr. Henry Vivier's recipe)

    2 pounds each boneless chuck and beef ribs
    4 chicken drumsticks or 1 goose neck
    ½ pound pork belly or slab bacon, cut in 1-inch strips
    ⅔ cup dried white beans
    1 parsnip, peeled and sliced
    1 bunch leeks, trimmed of root ends and tough green
       leaves, cut lengthwise and rinsed
    6 large carrots, peeled and sliced
    6 small onions, three of them stuck with a clove
    5 quarts cold water
    1 savoy cabbage, cored and cut in 8 wedges

Place all the ingredients except the cabbage in a large pot and cover with cold water. Let simmer for 4 to 6 hours without skimming.

Cook the cabbage separately for 10 minutes in boiling water. Place it in the pot of broth and let it sit until it is cool.

Strain the soup and chill it. Reserve the cabbage. Remove solidified fat from the top of the soup.

To serve, reheat the soup with the cabbage. This soup has to be perfect—that is, it has to be clear and flavorful.

Serves 8.

Boeuf à la Mode — *Braised Beef*

4 pounds beef rump roast, top or bottom round, or
  boneless chuck
1 pound spareribs, cut in 8 pieces
1 calf's foot [order this a few days before needed, from
  your butcher]
1 onion, cut in half crosswise, browned in a teaspoon
  of oil in a frying pan
2 tablespoons sugar
  Salt and freshly ground black pepper
¾ cup *eau-de-vie* or cognac
2 cups water
1 pound carrots, peeled and sliced
1 10-ounce box pearl onions, peeled (see Glossary,
  page 263)

Tenderize the beef by beating it with a mallet — or hit it with a
heavy frying pan or saucepan. Place the beef in a casserole with
the spareribs, calf's foot, browned onion, sugar, salt and pepper, *eau-de-vie,* and water.

Cover and cook slowly for 4 hours over a very low fire, turning
the meat every now and again.

Add the carrots in the last hour and the pearl onions in the last
20 minutes. Don't put them in too soon or they will melt into
the juices.

To serve hot: Skim off the fat before serving.

Place the beef on a platter with the onions on one side and the
carrots on the other; pour the juices over it.

To serve cold: Place some of the cooked carrots, in a decorative
manner, in the bottom of a mold 5 inches wide, 3 inches deep,
and 9 inches long. Pour in strained stock to cover them. Eat the

spareribs later; discard the calf's foot. Now slice the meat, against the grain, and fill the mold with the beef slices placed upright, the rest of the carrots, and more stock to cover. Refrigerate overnight. The next day you will find that the cold beef and carrots have jelled into a beautiful dish that is both appetizing and flavorful.

Unmold the beef and carrots before serving and garnish with the small onions or a bunch of watercress.

Serves 8.

Spoon-Tender Beef

The meat must be so tender that it need not be carved. It should be served with a spoon.

4	pounds beef rump roast or boneless chuck
2	tablespoons unsalted butter
¼	cup cognac
¼	cup Madeira
1	cup dry white wine
	Salt and freshly ground black pepper
10	medium-size onions, peeled
1	garlic clove, peeled
1	clove
8	sprigs fresh thyme, 1 bay leaf, and 4 parsley sprigs tied together
½	calf's foot [order this a few days before needed, from your butcher]
2 to 4	cups beef stock—4 cups will obviate the need to baste the beef
4	carrots, peeled and sliced
1	tablespoon unsalted butter

Optional Garnish

8 lettuce hearts, braised, 1 pound peas, or 8 artichoke bottoms

Brown the beef in the butter in a casserole over moderate heat. When it is golden, throw in the cognac, Madeira, white wine, and some salt and pepper. Bring to a boil.

Add the onions, garlic, and clove; the bouquet of thyme, bay leaf, and parsley; and the calf's foot and the stock. Cover and simmer gently for 5 hours, basting the meat often.

After 4 hours, brown the carrots in a little butter and add them to the casserole. Uncover during the last hour to reduce the broth to a sauce.

In the meantime, cook some vegetables that you would like as garnish (lettuce and peas or artichoke bottoms will go well) in water or vegetable stock. Arrange them around the beef on a large platter.

Before serving, skim the fat from the broth. Baste the vegetables generously with the broth.

Serves 8.

Chicken Fricassee with Pearl Onions

Chicken fricassee has to be white. In order to make a good fricassee, you must find a chicken fed on grain—a large roaster, not a skinny chicken. If you wish, you can add mushrooms, artichoke bottoms, or salsifys, cooked separately, or slices of truffle. Or you can make it a more elaborate dish by placing blanched brains and sweetbreads around the chicken. These can only enhance the dish.

1   4- to 5-pound roasting chicken, and its giblets
5   tablespooons unsalted butter
    Salt and freshly ground black pepper
½   cup all-purpose flour
4   cups hot water
1   bay leaf
1   2-inch-wide piece of lemon zest
    Salt and freshly ground black pepper
8   grinds nutmeg
3   sprigs thyme or 2 stems parsley
1   10-ounce box pearl onions, peeled (see Glossary,
    page 263)
1   large egg yolk
1   lemon, sliced

Prepare the chicken as if you were going to roast it. Put the liver in the cavity of the chicken with 1½ tablespoons butter, salt, and pepper and then truss it.

That done, place the chicken in a casserole over low heat with 3½ tablespoons butter. When the butter begins to melt, add the flour and stir it in. Add the hot water to half cover the chicken. Stir the liquid with a wooden spoon until it thickens.

When the water comes to a boil, turn the chicken on its side.

Add the bay leaf, lemon zest, salt, pepper, nutmeg, and don't forget the thyme or parsley.

Cover the casserole with a round of parchment paper and a close-fitting lid. Cook gently for 45 minutes.

Turn the chicken to the other side and add the peeled onions.

After another 45 minutes cooking, place the chicken on a platter, having strained the sauce.

Carve the chicken.

If the sauce looks too thin, first remove the onions and place them around the chicken. Boil the sauce, stirring all the time. When it has reduced enough, mix the egg yolk with a table-spoon of cold water. Then add ½ cup sauce, and whisk this back into the main sauce. Heat slowly for 1 minute until it thickens, but do not allow it to boil. Pour it over the chicken, which should be perfectly white and wonderful tasting.

Place slices of lemon around the edge of the platter.

Serves 6.

Ragouts — Stews

A good ragout, or stew, whether it is made of veal or lamb, should be well browned, aromatic, and served scorching hot. The sauce must be a thick blend of wonderful flavors. How few ragouts, alas, resemble this definition. What sad, tepid, badly made ragouts are so often served to us! They are so bad that you want to throw the dish and the cook out the window and take refuge in an Egyptian dessert of grilled locusts served with bread and honey, which would console you.

A good ragout is not very difficult to make—in fact it is simple—but you must give it loving care. You are sure to be successful if you follow this recipe exactly.

Lamb and Bean Ragout

¾ pound red or white dried beans or 3 12-ounce cans cooked beans
1½ to 2 pounds thick lamb chops or lamb neck, cut in 1½-inch cubes
2 tablespoons unsalted butter
12 medium onions, peeled

    2   tablespoons all-purpose flour
2 to 3   cups beef stock, or 1 beef bouillon cube diluted in 2 to
       3 cups water
    1   *bouquet garni* (see Glossary, page 259)
       Salt and freshly ground black pepper

Cook the dried beans in a pot of simmering water until tender, which takes up to 3 hours.

Sear the meat in 1 tablespoon butter in a frying pan over high heat, and when all the pieces are brown, remove them to a casserole.

Brown the onions with another tablespoon of butter in the empty frying pan, and add to the meat. Sprinkle with the flour. Shake the casserole, or stir, to disperse the flour and continue to cook gently for 5 minutes.

Add the stock, the *bouquet garni,* and salt and pepper.

Cover the casserole. Cook the ragout for 1½ hours, *at least,* at a constant simmer.

Add the beans to the ragout in the last 15 minutes so they take on good flavor.

Serve the ragout in a deep dish with the meat in the middle and the beans and sauce surrounding it. Don't forget to remove the *bouquet garni* before serving.

Serves 6.

Navarin — *A Lamb Stew*

Veal Ragout *Jardinière* is made in exactly the same way but it needs less cooking time. Veal is more tender and tends to fall apart if overcooked.

1 to 1½ pounds thick shoulder lamb chops [or lamb neck cut
in 1½-inch cubes]
2 tablespoons unsalted butter
6 carrots, peeled and sliced
6 turnips, peeled and cubed
1 teaspoon sugar
½ cup fresh peas
12 small onions, peeled
12 small potatoes, peeled
2 tablespoons all-purpose flour
2 cups beef stock, or 1 beef bouillon cube diluted in
2 cups water
1 *bouquet garni* (see Glossary, page 259)

Brown the lamb in 1 tablespoon butter in a frying pan. Place
the meat, when brown, in a casserole. Brown the vegetables
with the other tablespoon butter. Add the sugar. When the vegetables are browned, add them to the meat.

Sprinkle and stir the flour into the meat and vegetables.
Moisten with stock, and add salt and pepper and the *bouquet
garni.* Cover the casserole and let simmer for 1½ hours. Add the
peas, onions, and potatoes in the last ½ hour.

Serves 6.

Stuffed Cabbage

Stuffed cabbage is misunderstood; it is scorned; it is accused of
being indigestible; it is treated like a poor relative. It is rarely
placed on a menu when there are guests, which is quite unfair. A
well-made stuffed cabbage is a gift from the gods. It looks beautiful; its succulent leaves leave nothing to be desired, and, when
cooked long enough, it does not weigh on the stomach like a
rock. Here is an excellent recipe that will assure you of success.

  1 lovely, large savoy cabbage
     Cold water to cover
  6 ounces each ground veal and pork
 12 ounces chicken, finely chopped
  4 thick slices bacon
 ½ pound mushrooms, finely chopped
  2 tablespoons unsalted butter
     Salt and freshly ground black pepper
  4 pounds spinach, stalks removed and leaves rinsed
     twice
  1 pound bones, such as pork spareribs
  3 quarts chicken or beef stock or 6 chicken or beef
     bouillon cubes diluted in 3 quarts water
     Cheesecloth

Optional Garnish

  1 pound chipolatas — small cocktail frankfurters or
     sausages
 ¾ pound chestnuts, peeled and broiled
  1 pound button mushrooms, sautéed

Place the cabbage in a pot of water. Bring it to a boil and cook
for 20 minutes, until you see it open up like a large rose in full
bloom. (You can't separate the leaves when it is raw without
breaking them.) Let stand for 40 minutes.

In the meantime, make a stuffing with ground veal and pork,
chicken, 1 thick slice bacon, mushrooms, and salt and pepper.
All the ingredients must be ground or finely chopped, lightly
sautéed in butter, and seasoned well.

Cook the spinach separately and *squeeze it dry very thoroughly.*

When the cabbage is in bloom, drain it and begin delicately to
stuff leaf after leaf, leaving some of the outer leaves unstuffed.

Alternate a layer of stuffing under one leaf and a layer of spinach under another leaf, a layer of stuffing, and so on.

When the cabbage has been completely stuffed it will be a swollen version of its original shape. Wrap and tie it in cheesecloth.

Line a pot with 3 thick slices bacon and the bones. Place the cabbage in the pot and add the stock. Cover the pot and let it cook. The stock need not be a rich one; it will get stronger as it cooks.

Bring it to a boil and simmer for 1 hour. Remove the cabbage from the cheesecloth and remove the outer unstuffed leaves. Degrease the stock and reduce.

Before serving, reheat the cabbage in a low oven. Pour over the reduced sauce.

Optional Garnish: Chipolatas (heated in the sauce for 3 minutes) alternating with broiled chestnuts and mushrooms.

Serves 8 to 10.

Game

There is no finer game than in France. Hares, partridges, quail, and pheasants are depicted very favorably in our fables and famous stories, and one might say that they live up to their excellent reputation by being as tasty as they can be.

Don't talk to me about imported hares from Germany or Hungary, where the marshes have been infested for many years. Those overgrown hares are tasteless and may turn you away from that marvelous dish *Civet de Lièvre* (Hare Ragout, page 34).

And don't talk to me about those partridges, served in certain restaurants, that have been bred in aviaries. They have been fed on cabbage seeds, which makes their flesh black and oily, and they taste like a candle that has just been extinguished. A free-range partridge, that has the run of the Sologne plains, knows fear and thirst. It picks seeds from various fields, and it has altogether another flavor.

Water game birds such as wild ducks, pintail ducks, lapwings, plovers, and so on, are not very recommendable. However carefully prepared, they retain a wild taste and smell of fish. In general, pheasant, partridge, quail, and even lark are best roasted on a spit with whatever sauce you prefer. It is best to roast them over a wood fire, or at least over live coals. You can wrap these birds with a fine sheet of lard (thin sheets of fat can be bought from the butcher). It is best to wrap quail in grape leaves.

Don't forget to put a thick slice of stale bread under the bird when you cook it. This slice of bread soaks up the juices and becomes delicious. (Do not toast the bread beforehand, because it will dry out and you won't be able to crack it with your teeth.)

Pheasant can be served with a garnish of roasted chestnuts, red cabbage, or thin slices of fried bacon.

Quail only take 10 to 12 minutes to cook. You must eat them scorching hot. A drop of blood should form on the skin when you cut into them. Wrapping grape leaves around quail imparts an especially good flavor to them.

Quail Risotto

Here is another way to cook quail that is very good.

    2   ounces (½ stick) unsalted butter
    2   shallots, finely chopped
    4   1-inch pieces marrow bone—use only the marrow
    1   small onion, finely chopped

2   cups Arborio (Italian-style) rice
5   cups hot light chicken or beef stock (or a mixture) or
    4 chicken or beef stock cubes diluted in 5 cups water
¼   cup grated Gruyère cheese
    Salt and freshly ground black pepper

Roasted Quail

1 or 2   quail per person
         Salt and freshly ground black pepper
         Sage or thyme sprigs
         Oil

Preheat the oven to 400 degrees.

Place the butter in a frying pan and add shallots and marrow. Let them cook over low heat without browning. Push this mixture through a strainer over a saucepan—the flavored butter is used to make the risotto. Add a finely chopped white onion to the saucepan and cook over moderate to low heat until tender, but not browned. Add the rice and stir. After a few minutes, add 3 cups of hot stock.

Continue to cook over low heat. Stir the rice as necessary to prevent it from sticking to the bottom of the pan.

When the stock has been absorbed, add one more cup of stock. Add salt and pepper. Add more stock and cook until it has been absorbed. The risotto takes about 40 minutes to cook. Cooked by this method, each grain of rice remains whole. When you take the saucepan off the heat, stir in the grated Gruyère.

In the meantime, sprinkle the cavities of the quail with salt and pepper and add some sprigs of a fresh herb such as sage or thyme. Tie the quail into neat round bundles. Sauté the quail in oil in a frying pan until browned all over, then finish cooking them in a baking pan for 10 minutes in the oven when the risotto is nearly finished. Don't forget to remove the strings before serving.

Place the risotto on a platter with the roast quail on top. Everyone is certain to be satisfied with this meal.

Serves 4.

Civet de Lièvre — *Hare Ragout*

A true civet *can only be made when you are somewhere where hare abound. Use a large rabbit as an alternative.*

  1   young hare or large rabbit, weighing 4 to 5 pounds
  2   tablespoons unsalted butter
  2   ounces pork belly or 4 thick slices bacon, chopped
20   small onions, peeled
  2   tablespoons all-purpose flour
  3   cups chicken stock or 2 chicken stock cubes diluted
      in 3 cups water
  1   large *bouquet garni* (see Glossary, page 259)
      Salt and freshly ground black pepper
  2   cups red wine

Cut the hare or rabbit into 10 pieces with a knife — don't use a cleaver because the bones will splinter.

Melt the butter in a large sauté pan over moderate heat. Fry the pork belly in it and put aside. Brown the pieces of hare in the same butter and place them in a casserole. Brown the onions in the same butter again and put aside.

Stir the flour into the butter and cook for 2 minutes. Add the stock and stir (thereby making a *roux*), and pour it over the hare. Add the pork belly, a large *bouquet garni*, and salt and pepper.

Simmer gently for 1 to 1¼ hours. Add the small onions and red wine in the last ½ hour.

Serves 6.

Rabbit, Hunter-Style

 1 3-pound rabbit, cut in 8 pieces
 2 tablespoons unsalted butter
 Salt and freshly ground black pepper
 ½ teaspoon *quatre épices* (see Glossary, page 263)
 10 ounces button mushrooms, sliced
 1 tablespoon each parsley and tarragon, chopped
 1 shallot, minced
 1½ cups dry white wine

Place the pieces of rabbit in a casserole with the butter, salt and pepper, and *quatre épices*. Sauté them over moderate heat until they have browned. Add the mushrooms, parsley, tarragon, minced shallot, and white wine.

Bring to a boil, lower the heat and simmer, covered, for 45 minutes.

Serves 4.

Pheasant à la Sainte-Alliance,
from La Physiologie du Goût *by Brillat-Savarin*

Brillat-Savarin says, "This fine-tasting bird must be basted with, preferably, a young wine from *haute* Burgundy; I came to this conclusion after a series of observances that cost me more work than a logarithm table. A pheasant prepared this way is a dish to serve to angels, if they are still traveling on earth as in the time of Loth."

2	woodcocks, gutted, entrails saved
4	pieces beef marrow 1½ inch long, steamed
3	tablespoons grated bacon fat
	Salt and freshly ground black pepper
	Fines herbes (see Glossary, page 261)
2 to 3	truffles, chopped [or 1 pound button mushrooms, quartered and sautéed in fat]
1	pheasant
2	slices bread, fried in unsalted butter
1	anchovy
1	tablespoon unsalted butter

Garnish: sections of 2 bitter [blood, or navel] oranges

Bone the woodcocks and use the flesh to make a filling by chopping it with the steamed beef marrow, bacon, salt and pepper, *fines herbes*, and all but 2 tablespoons truffles or mushrooms, to fill a pheasant.

Stuff the pheasant. Use 1 slice of fried bread to act as a stop cock to keep the stuffing from spilling out. Tie up the pheasant.

Preheat the oven to 400 degrees.

Take the liver and entrails of the woodcocks and finely chop them with the rest of the truffle or mushrooms, anchovy, bacon, and butter. Spread this paste on the remaining fried bread, or crouton.

Place the pheasant on the crouton so the juices are absorbed by it.

Roast the pheasant for 45 minutes, first on one side, then the other, then the back, for 15 minutes on each side.

When the pheasant is cooked, serve it breast up on the crouton, surrounded with bitter oranges. Be as calm as you can before this event.

Serves 2 to 4.

Simple Omelet

You can vary the omelets infinitely. Add mushrooms, truffles, herring, bacon, and so on. But the principle remains the same. If you adhere to these instructions you will always obtain a moist golden omelet that is not too runny. For an omelet to be successful, it should not be too large: 8 to 10 eggs is sufficient. If you use more, it will be difficult to cook.

8 to 10	large eggs
2	tablespoons milk
	Salt and freshly ground black pepper
3	tablespoons unsalted butter

Break the eggs into a bowl. Add the milk and very little salt and pepper. Whisk the mixture for a few minutes.

Melt the butter in a 12-inch frying pan over moderate heat. When the butter is hot and golden brown, pour the eggs into the frying pan.

After 30 seconds the eggs will be partially cooked underneath. Tilt the frying pan and lift up the edge of the eggs with a fork, letting the uncooked eggs run underneath. Continue to cook, repeating this operation until the whole omelet is cooked.

Fold the omelet, slide it onto a hot platter, and serve.

The total cooking time should not be more than 5 minutes.

Serves 4.

Potato Salad

Potato salad is a veritable institution. It is rare that it is properly made. Cooks ignore tradition or they misunderstand the principles and the result is lamentable—the connoisseur of potato salad is the victim. I present this recipe somewhat timidly, because it may not be the whole story, but I will give a few explanations that come from a long family tradition.

Potato salad has to be made with Dutch potatoes that are ivory colored, tight, and compact—when sliced, they keep their shape perfectly and do not break apart. When making potato salad, you must *steam the potatoes whole.* Do not boil them as is usually done.

There is a very simple way to steam potatoes. Use a round rack a little smaller than the diameter of a *marmite* or 8-quart stockpot. Put the rack inside the *marmite* halfway up, making sure that it doesn't drop to the bottom. Fix the sides of the rack with some wire (they sell racks for just such a purpose). If you do not possess one of these racks, you can replace it with little pieces of wood placed one on top of each other, this way and that, like a bird's nest. In any case, whether you use a rack or the little pieces of wood, you need to place the potatoes above the water so that they are cooked only by the steam.

Note: The simplest thing to do is to buy a *marmite* with a steamer container on top from any large shop. They cost about 6 francs—well worth the expense. [You can use any steamer receptacle and pot combination.]

  1 pound small red bliss potatoes
  2 tablespoons red wine vinegar—preferably homemade, aged wine vinegar
  ¼ teaspoon salt
 10 grinds black pepper
  3 tablespoons olive oil
    Pinch cayenne pepper
  1 pickled herring fillet or 3 anchovy fillets marinated in olive oil with thin rounds of 1 small onion

Steam the potatoes for 10 to 15 minutes—avoid overcooking them.

Make a vinaigrette by whisking together the vinegar, salt and pepper, olive oil, and cayenne pepper. Add the herring or anchovy fillets and onions and blend. When the potatoes are cooked, peel them if you want and slice them quite thickly while they are still hot into the vinaigrette.

When the salad is well moistened with the vinaigrette, which will take about an hour, there should be no more vinaigrette left in the bottom of the bowl.

Now you can eat it—warm and delicious. You can reheat the salad before serving, but you must be careful not to overheat it.

Serves 4.

Royal Pudding à la Dutrait-Crozen

Start the preparation 2 weeks before needed.

2½	pounds plums
	Very old cognac, maraschino, or very old port to cover
1	cup rice, long grain
½	cup sugar
	Pinch salt
2	cups water
1	cup milk
1½	cups heavy cream
6	large egg whites

Cut the plums in half. Discard the seeds. Place the cut fruit in a jar full of very old cognac. Macerate for 2 weeks.

When the percolation is accomplished, cook the rice, sugar, and salt with the water and milk for 45 minutes over a very low fire. Place the rice in the food processor, add the cream, and process until nearly smooth.

Take a shallow dish and layer the plums and rice. Beat the egg whites stiff. Fashion an elegant mountain of beaten whites on top of the fruit.

Bake for 20 minutes in a 400-degree oven until the mountain is solid, cooked, and golden brown—like a meringue.

Eat it hot.

Serves 8.

Spices and Sauces

Salt, Pepper, Cayenne, Nutmeg, Cloves, Parsley, Chervil, Tarragon, Savory, Thyme, Bay Leaves, Cinnamon, Sel-Épices, Onions, and Garlic

Jus
Sauce Espagnole *or* Sauce Brune— *Spanish or Brown Sauce*
Tomato Sauce
Béarnaise Sauce
Hollandaise Sauce
Shrimp Sauce
Mousseline Sauce
Béchamel Sauce
Maître d'Hôtel *Sauce*
Ravigote *Sauce*
White Sauce
Rémoulade *Sauce*
Mayonnaise
Sauce Tartare
Sauce Poivrade— *Pepper-Vinegar Sauce*
Another Sauce Poivrade— *Pepper-Vinegar Sauce*
Piquant Sauce
Fish Stock and Variation: Coulis de Poisson— *Fish Sauce*
Matelote *Sauce—A Fish Sauce*

Cream Sauce	*Périgueux Sauce*
Chicken Stock	*Anchovy Butter*
Game Stock	*Shrimp Butter*
Salmis *Sauce*	*Three Horseradish Sauces*

Spices

Before talking about sauces, I want to enumerate the spices and condiments that are indispensable to any cook who deserves the title. Spices and condiments must *never* be missing in a household where eating well is important.

First of all, *salt:* raw (coarse salt) and fine salt. The best—I have already mentioned it in the recipe for Boiled Beef (page 17)—is from the salt marshes. It is in your interest to have 4 to 6 pounds sent from a spice merchant, either from Piriac, Bourge-de-Batz, Gúerande, Loire-Atlantique, or any other region where there are salt marshes. There is nothing like fresh salt. It is not impregnated with dust, nor is it dead; it still has the taste of the landscape in it. To really appreciate it, simply taste a few grains.

Fine salt must be kept away from dust, in covered jars in a dry place. Open one jar at a time.

Coarse salt should be kept in a little wooden trough with a hinged lid; this little trough should hang on a wall in the kitchen convenient to the cook.

Pepper must be bought in grain form from a good spice market. You should never buy pepper already ground—it's the color of sand. You must grind it yourself. Buy 2 to 4 ounces of peppercorns and remember to ask for a mixture of black and white pepper. You need to have two peppermills. One for the kitchen (and it must not leave the kitchen), and another for the dining room, which must be placed on the table at every meal.

A little jar of *cayenne pepper*, or red pepper, is also indispensable. This pepper is sold in powder form in small quantities. It is strong like the devil; use only a small amount each time.

Nutmeg. You need one to two nutmegs on hand, no more. The taste of this spice is very pronounced, so it must be used sparingly, nearly imperceptibly, to be agreeable. It must never dominate a dish. Grate a little each time it is needed. Keep the nutmeg in a separate box or jar so it will not contaminate the other spices.

Cloves. Cloves, which are often stuck into onions, must also be kept in a container away from dust. Be sparing with this spice.

Parsley, chervil, and *tarragon* can be bought in sufficient quantities to last two or three days, as long as you keep their stalks in a bowl of fresh water. Change the water every day. When they droop, they have lost their essential flavor.

Savory. This fragrant herb, hardly found anywhere except in Touraine, is finer than thyme and not as strong as mint. It dries well. You can make a large bouquet of it and keep it in a closet. It enhances vegetables and also pea soup.

Thyme and *bay leaves* can be kept the same way.

Cinnamon is best bought from chez Hédiard (27, place de la Madeleine). They sell it in a glass tube, like vanilla beans. It is expensive, but it lasts a long time, because you must use it with discretion.

Finally I want to give a recipe for *Sel-Épices*, or spiced salt, invented by the celebrated Chef Durand. It incorporates most of the aforementioned spices. Here is the recipe he gave to me. [Use it as you use salt, for extra flavor, in savory food.]

Sel-Épices

5 ounces salt
½ teaspoon ground cloves
4 tablespoons ground nutmeg
6 bay leaves, crumbled
3 tablespoons cinnamon
1 teaspoon black pepper
4 large dried basil leaves, crumbled
1 teaspoon ground coriander seed

Grind all ingredients [in a blender or coffee grinder]. After they have been ground together, pass them through a silk *tamis* (very fine sieve). If there is any residue left, place it in the mortar and grind it some more. To make sure the proportions are exact—the fruit of thousands of tests—nothing must be lost. You must pass the remains through the sieve. Blend the mixture when all is finely ground and sieved, and press it into a tin, which should be sealed hermetically.

Let me add that you must always have a small amount of *onions* and *garlic* on hand, stored in a dry place.

I strongly advise that you buy your garlic from the Midi—from Chabaz, rue de Vieux-Sextier, Avignon, Provence. You are assured of receiving the best. This garlic is not like any you can obtain in Paris or other regions of France. The garlic you buy in Paris is heavy and strong and it sends forth a terrible odor; it numbs the taste of the food you are eating. Garlic from Avignon is light and delicate and its odor evaporates quickly. Above all, if it is cooked well, it will never overwhelm—on the contrary, it will only improve—a dish. People from the south of France who eat *aioli* [garlic mayonnaise] smell of garlic because the garlic is pounded raw with the oil. Without having the audacity to eat *aioli*, you can add a touch of garlic to certain dishes and not annoy anyone. There are some dishes where the absence of garlic is a grave sin, such as eggplants, *cèpes*, stuffed tomatoes, and so on.

Sauces

I am going to group all the sauces together instead of scattering them throughout the book, mostly because it will be easier to find them. Also, most of them are used in all the regions of France, and it would be arbitrary to relegate any of them to one region. Doubtless there are differences between a tomato sauce made in Lille and a tomato sauce made in Avignon. The same goes for a béarnaise or mayonnaise. But the basic method by which these sauces are prepared remains the same, and it is on the foundation of these unchanging principles that I give the recipes.

Jus

Jus, indispensable and basic to good cooking, improves nearly all sauces. It can be made and stored without costing much, if you are an economical cook who knows how to use leftovers.

Pieces of leftover meat, veal or beef bones, or leg of lamb bone with a little meat still clinging to it can make an excellent *jus*. Use as a glaze with all meat dishes.

8   cups leftover meat, assorted cracked bones
3   chicken drumsticks
½   pound salt pork
3   carrots, peeled and sliced
2   turnips, peeled and cubed
2   medium onions, sliced
1   bay leaf

1   clove garlic, smashed
    Salt
1   tablespoon pork fat, chicken fat, or unsalted butter
1   pinch sugar
6   cups water

Place leftover meat or cracked bones and drumsticks in a large
pot with salt pork, carrots, turnips, onions, bay leaf, garlic, and
salt. Anoint this with pork fat, chicken fat, or butter. Brown
the meats and vegetables over moderate heat. Don't forget a
pinch of sugar to help the ingredients take on color.

At first you have to stir the bottom of the saucepan so that the
vegetables do not burn. When the vegetables and meat are
brown, add the water and simmer for 2 to 3 hours.

Strain the *jus* and, according to your needs, reduce it to make a
sauce, or leave as a thin broth.

If you are going to keep it chilled in the refrigerator, bring it to
a boil every few days. You can keep this *jus* for 8 to 10 days.

Yield: 3 cups.

Sauce Espagnole *or* Sauce Brune—
Spanish or Brown Sauce

[This recipe does not resemble the traditional recipe at all.]

I have to admit that I don't like this sauce very much. I feel that
it masks the taste of the meat [because of the ham in it, per-
haps]. However, it is traditional to French cuisine, and I cannot
help but give the recipe. Use with steaks, poached eggs or ham
dishes.

¾   pound ham, cubed
3   chicken drumsticks

1 medium onion, roughly chopped
1 carrot, peeled and finely sliced
¼ cup fat from the ham, cubed
1 cup dry white wine
2 thick slices lemon
4 cups cold water
1 *bouquet garni* (see Glossary, page 259)
1 clove garlic, smashed

Place the ham, drumsticks, onion, carrot, and fat from the ham in a saucepan and brown all. Moisten with the dry white wine, lemon slices, water, *bouquet garni,* and garlic. Simmer and reduce for 40 minutes.

Strain through a sieve, chill, and remove the fat. Refrigerate.

Yield: 2½ cups.

Tomato Sauce

Nowadays it is pretty rare that you can find a good tomato sauce—a thick, colorful sauce with the fresh scent of tomatoes. Three-quarters of the time you are served, under the name of tomato sauce, a pink acidic juice that smells of raw flour. It's only in Provence, the country of the *pomme d'amour,* that you can find a decent recipe for this excellent sauce. Use as a pasta sauce, with steaks, or vegetables such as eggplant.

2 ounces salt pork, diced
4 ounces ham, cubed
1 thick slice bacon, finely chopped
1 carrot, peeled and sliced
1 onion, finely chopped
12 medium tomatoes, halved and seeded
1 bay leaf

1   large clove garlic, minced
    Salt and freshly ground black pepper
2   cups chicken stock whisked into 2 tablespoons
    all-purpose flour

Cook the salt pork, ham, and bacon together in a saucepan over moderate heat until browned.

Add the carrot and onion and brown them also.

Add the tomatoes. Use a wooden spoon to stir and crush them.

Add the bay leaf, garlic, and salt and pepper. Cover the saucepan and simmer for 15 minutes.

Add the 2 cups of stock mixed with flour. Cook for another 20 minutes uncovered. Push through the fine mesh of a food mill. Cook the sauce further if you want to thicken it.

Yield: 2 quarts.

Note: Instead of using fresh tomatoes, you can use your own preserved or canned tomatoes. If you do so, make the following adjustments in the recipe:

2   cups chicken or beef stock
⅓   cup cold water whisked with 3 tablespoons flour
2   28-ounce cans tomatoes, seeded

Make a light *roux* (see Glossary, page 263) — use the stock and water mixed with flour. Add the tomatoes. Crush them with a wooden spoon. If the tomatoes have already been cooked and seasoned, add only a small amount of salt and pepper and cook for 30 minutes altogether.

Béarnaise Sauce

[This sauce is wonderful with steaks, eggs, vegetables, or fish.]

     2 shallots, minced
     1 *bouquet garni* of thyme, bay leaf, parsley, chervil,
        and tarragon (see Glossary, page 259)
    ½ cup white vinegar
     3 large egg yolks
    3½ ounces (1 stick less 1 tablespoon) unsalted butter,
        melted
        Salt and freshly ground black pepper
     1 tablespoon each chervil and tarragon, chopped or
        2 tablespoons tarragon

Place the shallots, *bouquet garni,* and vinegar in a saucepan. Cook them over moderate heat until the vinegar has just about completely reduced, about 5 minutes.

Remove the *bouquet garni,* lower the heat, whisk in the egg yolks, and add the warm melted butter little by little.

The sauce must thicken like a cream. Be very careful not to overheat — the least excess of heat will curdle the sauce. Add a pinch salt, a little pepper, chopped chervil, and tarragon.

Yield: 1½ cups.

Hollandaise Sauce

[Serve with poached eggs, steamed broccoli, or potatoes.]

     3 large egg yolks
    ½ pound unsalted butter, melted
        A few drops lemon juice
        Salt

Place 2 egg yolks in a saucepan and whisk in some of the melted butter over very low heat. Then add, whisking all the time, more butter until the sauce takes on a beautiful smooth consistency. Add a third egg yolk, a few drops lemon juice, and salt. Serve from a bowl or sauceboat.

Yield: 2 cups.

Shrimp Sauce

[Pour over poached, sautéed, or baked fish.]

Prepare a thick hollandaise and replace some of the butter with shrimp butter (see page 64).

Add some peeled shrimp at the last moment.

Mousseline Sauce

[Use this sauce as you would hollandaise—it is lovely on fish dishes or with *quenelles.*]

Follow the recipe for Hollandaise Sauce, but fold in ½ cup whipped cream (*crème chantilly* without the sugar) just before serving. The cream lightens the sauce and gives it a more delicate taste.

Béchamel Sauce

[This is an all-purpose white sauce to which other flavors can be added, such as cheese. Pour over macaroni or vegetable gratins.]

    3   tablespoons all-purpose flour
    1½ cups milk
        Salt and freshly ground black pepper

1 tablespoon parsley, chopped
5 grinds nutmeg or ⅛ teaspoon
   Pinch sugar
2 tablespoons unsalted butter
1 egg yolk

In a saucepan make a thin *bouillie* (a paste—see Glossary, page 259) with a mixture of milk and flour. Allow it to come to a boil, lower the heat and simmer for 10 minutes.

Add salt and pepper, chopped parsley, nutmeg, and sugar.

Then whisk in the butter and egg yolk. Heat slowly for 1 minute until it thickens, but do not allow to boil.

Yield: 1½ cups.

Another method, by Chef Durand:

5 tablespoons unsalted butter
2 tablespoons all-purpose flour
1½ cups hot milk
   Salt and freshly ground black pepper
1 carrot, peeled and sliced
1 small onion, stuck with a clove

In a saucepan make a white *roux* (see Glossary, page 263) with 4 tablespoons butter, flour, and boiling milk. Stir until it comes to a boil.

Season with salt and pepper, add the carrot and onion and bring to a boil again. Lower the heat and simmer until the sauce thickens, stirring frequently, for about 15 minutes.

Add 1 tablespoon butter and strain the sauce.

Yield: 1½ cups.

Maître d'Hôtel *Sauce*

[A flavored butter that goes well with steaks, fish, and poultry.]

    4   ounces (1 stick) unsalted butter, softened
    ¼   teaspoon salt
        Freshly ground black pepper
    2   tablespoons parsley, finely chopped
    2   teaspoons lemon juice

Melt the butter in a saucepan and add the rest of the ingredients.

[To keep: cool the butter, shape into a log shape, wrap in plastic wrap and refrigerate. When needed cut slices to melt on top of steaks, and so on.]

Yield: ½ cup flavored butter.

Ravigote *Sauce*

[This is a delicious accompaniment to chilled fish, mussels, and shrimp.]

    2   large hard-boiled eggs—use only the yolks
    4   anchovy fillets
    ¼   cup extra-virgin olive oil
    2   tablespoons red wine vinegar
    2   tablespoons Dijon mustard
        Salt and freshly ground pepper
    2   tablespoons *fines herbes* (see Glossary, page 261),
        finely chopped

Pound or process the hard-cooked egg yolks and anchovies together. Place the mixture in a bowl and pour olive oil very slowly onto the yolk mixture, whisking all the time. Add the vinegar, mustard, and salt and pepper.

Finally, add the *fines herbes* and serve from a sauceboat.

Yield: nearly 1 cup.

White Sauce

[This is an excellent fine white sauce to accompany fish and vegetables.]

>6 tablespoons unsalted butter
>2 tablespoons all-purpose flour
>1 cup water
>2 teaspoons lemon juice
>5 grinds nutmeg or ⅛ teaspoon
>½ teaspoon salt
>2 tablespoons [nonpareil] capers (optional)
>½ teaspoon lemon juice or vinegar (optional)

Melt 4 tablespoons butter in a saucepan, over moderate heat. Stir in the flour and gradually add the water, lemon juice, nutmeg, and salt.

Bring to a simmer; let cook 10 minutes. Take the sauce off the fire and add 2 tablespoons butter, stirring until it melts, but without boiling. Serve.

If you wish you may add capers and vinegar or lemon juice a few moments before serving.

Yield: 1½ cups.

Rémoulade *Sauce*

[This enriched mayonnaise is fine with fish, cold meats, and poultry.]

 2 large egg yolks
    Salt and freshly ground black pepper
 3 tablespoons minced shallots
 2 tablespoons finely chopped tarragon
 ½ cup olive oil
 1 tablespoon mustard
 2 tablespoons finely chopped cornichons
 1 tablespoon red wine vinegar

Place egg yolks in a bowl with salt, pepper, shallots, and tarragon.

Whisk in the olive oil little by little. Stir in mustard, cornichons, and vinegar.

Yield: 1 cup.

Mayonnaise

[This all-purpose mayonnaise is used in poultry, fish, and vegetable salads.]

It is a good idea to make this sauce in a cool place. Or better still, in hot weather place the bowl inside another bowl containing ice. This way you can be sure that it will not curdle.

 2 large egg yolks—be sure to remove the stringy parts
    [chalazas] of the egg whites
 1 cup olive oil
    Salt and freshly ground black pepper
 1 teaspoon vinegar

Place the yolks in a bowl and stir with a wooden spoon or whisk. Add olive oil little by little; stir continuously with a uniform movement so as to clean the sides of the bowl regularly.

When the mayonnaise begins to thicken, you can add the oil at a faster rate.

Season the mayonnaise with salt and pepper and vinegar.

Yield: just over 1 cup.

Sauce Tartare

This sauce is excellent with broiled eel [fried fish, and shellfish dishes].

> 1 recipe Mayonnaise (page 56)
> 2 shallots, finely chopped
> 1 tablespoon each finely chopped chervil and tarragon
> 2 tablespoons each chopped cornichons and capers
>   Pinch cayenne pepper

Stir all the ingredients in the mayonnaise and add cayenne pepper to garnish.

Yield: 1½ cups.

Sauce Poivrade — *Pepper-Vinegar Sauce*

[This spicy, acidic sauce is a good accompaniment to fish or meat steaks.]

> 6 parsley sprigs
> 3 scallions, chopped
> 1 bay leaf

  1 slice of onion
  ½ cup vinegar
  15 peppercorns
     Salt
  ¾ cup glaze — reduced *jus* (see page 47)

Place parsley sprigs, scallions, bay leaf, onion, vinegar, pepper-corns, and salt in a saucepan.

Bring to a boil over high heat and reduce for 6 minutes. Add a little glaze (that is to say *jus* that you have reduced) and let boil 5 minutes.

Degrease the sauce if necessary and strain through a sieve.

Yield: 1 cup.

Another Sauce Poivrade — *Pepper-Vinegar Sauce*

Serve this sauce with a piece of game such as fillet or haunch of venison or fillet of beef.

  1 fillet (tenderloin) or haunch (ham) of venison
  1 teaspoon crushed black peppercorns
  ½ cup vinegar
  2 shallots, minced
  1 cup stock
  ½ cup red Bordeaux wine
  3 tablespoons fine bread crumbs or finely ground almonds

After the game is roasted, add the crushed peppercorns, vin-egar, and minced shallots to the pan.

Let reduce completely, then add the stock and Bordeaux.

Reduce further, then bind the sauce with the bread crumbs or almonds.

Yield: 1½ cups.

Piquant Sauce

This is not a famous sauce, but it always enhances leftover chicken or meats.

- 4 tablespoons unsalted butter
- 2 tablespoons all-purpose flour
- 1 cup beef or chicken stock
- 5 shallots, minced
  Salt and freshly ground black pepper
- 1 *bouquet garni* (see Glossary, page 259)
- 1 clove
- 5 cornichons, sliced
- 1 tablespoon vinegar

Make a thin, light *roux* (see Glossary, page 263) with the butter, flour, and stock in a saucepan over moderate heat. Add the shallots, salt, pepper, a *bouquet garni,* and the clove. Simmer for 20 minutes. Add sliced cornichons and vinegar.

Yield: 1 cup.

Fish Stock and Variation:
Coulis de Poisson—*Fish Sauce*

- 2 tablespoons unsalted butter
  Heads, skin, and bones of 3 flounder, fluke, red snapper, sole, or other white-fleshed fish
- 1 onion, sliced

    1   carrot, sliced
        Water

Place the butter, onion, and carrot in a saucepan. Sauté the vegetables without browning them. Add fish heads, skin, and bones. Add water to cover and bring to a boil.

Simmer for about 20 minutes, or until the flesh falls off the bones. Strain.

To make a *Coulis de Poisson*—light fish sauce—to accompany broiled or baked fish, thicken the stock with a light *roux* (see Glossary, page 263) that you have made separately.

Yield: about 4 cups.

Matelote *Sauce—A Fish Sauce*

    2   tablespoon unsalted butter
    1   cup fish stock
    2   tablespoons *crème fraîche* (see Glossary, page 260)

Melt the butter in a saucepan. Add the fish stock and then the *crème fraîche*. Cook for 10 to 15 minutes.

Yield: 1 cup.

Cream Sauce—To Go with Everything

   ¼   cup heavy cream
    4   tablespoons unsalted butter
        Salt and freshly ground black pepper

Heat the butter and cream in a double boiler or over very low heat, whisking often for 20 minutes. Add salt and pepper.

Serve this sauce with eggs or fish. This sauce goes with everything; it is delicious.

Yield: ½ cup.

Chicken Stock

[This stock has innumerable uses, primarily for soups and sauces.]

 2 chicken carcasses or 5 chicken legs
    Giblets
 1 carrot, sliced
 2 shallots, sliced
 1 clove
    Cold water

Place the carcasses, giblets, a carrot, shallots, and a clove in a saucepan. Add water to cover by 2 inches; bring to a boil and skim.

Simmer on a low fire until the flesh is falling off the bones, about 1½ hours. Strain the stock through a sieve.

Yield: 1 quart.

Game Stock

Prepare exactly as in the preceding recipe, but replace the chicken carcasses with pheasant, young rabbit, or partridge carcasses or bones.

Salmis *Sauce*

Woodcocks, wild ducks, teal, or pintail ducks are excellent prepared with this sauce. Serve a wonderful old bottle of red Burgundy with this dish. Burgundy is the companion and friend
to strong game.

> 2 tablespoons unsalted butter
> 2 tablespoons flour
> 2 cups chicken stock
> 1 liver of the game bird, crushed [or 3 tablespoons fine
>   bread crumbs or finely ground almonds]
> 1 *bouquet garni* (see Glossary, page 259)
>   Salt and freshly ground black pepper
>   Bones and scraps of meat from game birds
> 1½ cups red wine

In a large pot, make a *roux* (see Glossary, page 263) using
the butter, flour, and stock. Add the crushed liver, the *bouquet
garni*, salt, and pepper.

Add the carcasses and scraps of meat that you want for flavor.

Boil for 20 minutes, then add the red wine and simmer for 30
minutes more. Discard the *bouquet garni* and the bones.

Yield: 2 cups.

To make a *salmis*:

> 1 wild duck or 2 woodcocks
> 8 slices baguette, fried in butter
> 2 tablespoons olive oil

Roast the game halfway. Add to the sauce. Cook without letting it boil, until heated through.

Place fried bread slices on a platter with the pieces of game on top.

Beat the olive oil into the sauce. Pour over the game.

Serve hot, eat hot.

Serves 2.

Périgueux Sauce

Serve this delicious sauce with a fillet of beef, cooked *à point* (medium rare), surrounded with little rounds of brioche.

  2 tablespoons unsalted butter
  2 tablespoons all-purpose flour
1½ cups beef stock
  1 cup Madeira
     Pan juices
  3 truffles, finely chopped [or 2 tablespoons Salsa
     Tartufata or 1 tablespoon white truffle oil]
     Salt and freshly ground black pepper

In a saucepan, make a *roux* (see Glossary, page 263) using the butter, flour, and stock. Add the Madeira. Reduce over a low fire for 40 minutes.

Before serving with roast meat, add the pan juices, chopped truffles, and salt and pepper.

Yield: 1½ cups.

Anchovy Butter

[This butter is fine with sardines or other grilled or broiled fish. It is also useful as a spread on canapés.]

       6   salted anchovy fillets [or in oil]
       4   ounces (1 stick) unsalted butter, softened
           A few drops of lemon juice

[Process the anchovies, butter, and lemon juice in a food processor.

Shape the Anchovy Butter into a log and wrap in plastic. Refrigerate or freeze.

Melt slices of Anchovy Butter on fish, meat, or bread.

Yield: a little more than 4 ounces flavored butter.]

Shrimp Butter

[This sauce is delicious swirled into a fish soup at the end of cooking. It can also be used as a spread on canapés.]

       4   ounces small shrimp
      3½   ounces unsalted butter
           Salt and freshly ground black pepper

Process the shrimp and butter together. When a paste has been formed, heat it on the stove, stirring with a wooden spoon.

When the butter has melted and clarified, it will turn golden— 5 to 10 minutes. Strain it through cheesecloth or a fine sieve, squeezing it until you have extracted all the butter.

Store the shrimp butter in the refrigerator or freezer.

Yield: 2 ounces flavored butter.

Three Horseradish Sauces

I. *Cold Horseradish,*
   to serve with Beef in the Pot-au-Feu, *page 14.*

   ¼   cup grated horseradish
   ½   teaspoon salt
       Freshly ground black pepper
   2   tablespoons olive oil
   2   tablespoons vinegar
   ¼   cup hot beef stock

Mix all the ingredients together.

Chill.

Yield: ¾ cup.

II. *Horseradish Sauce,*
    to serve with Roast Leg of Lamb

   2   cups heavy cream
   2½   ounces grated horseradish
         Salt

Boil the cream until reduced by half.

Let cool and add grated horseradish and a pinch of salt.

Yield: 1¼ cups.

III. *Another Horseradish Sauce,*
     to serve with plain Roast Beef

   2   tablespoons unsalted butter
   1   tablespoon all-purpose flour
   1   cup beef stock
   ¾   cup fresh bread crumbs
   1¼   cups grated horseradish

Melt the butter in a saucepan over moderate heat.

Add the flour and stir.

Add the stock and stir until smooth.

Lastly stir in the bread crumbs and horseradish.

Heat for 1 minute and serve.

Yield: 2½ cups.

II
Regional Dishes

FRENCH FLANDERS
Sauce for Roast Hare
Thrush

ILE DE FRANCE
French Fries
Petits Pois Parisienne
Langouste Parisienne
Lobster Bourg-la-Reine
Rice à l'Indienne
Veal Terrine Armenonville
Chicken Franchard
Veal Scallops Franchard
Fried Gudgeons
La Matelote — *Freshwater Fish Stew*
Entrecôte *Bercy* — *Grilled Beef Steak*
Fried Entrecôte *Bercy*
Rich Macaroni
Crepes Mollettes — *Soft Delicate Crepes*
Leon Daudet's Crepes

TOURAINE
Fava Beans Tourangelle
Green Walnuts

ORLEANS
Grilled Herring
Jellied Carp
Hare à la Royale

PERCHE
Tripe à la Mode d'Authon du Perche

POITOU
Cheese Tourte

CHAMPAGNE
Turkey or Chicken Champenois

NORMANDY
Norman Fat
Soup Made with Fat
Onion and Potato Soup
Norman Sole
Boeuf à la Mode de Caen — *Braised Beef*
Duck Rouennaise
Tripe à la Mode de Caen
Fried Steak
Matelote *Sole*
Sautéed Rabbit with Carrots and Onions
Norman Sauce for Roast Rabbit
Broiled Mushrooms
La Terrinée — *Rice Pudding*
Le Beau Ténébreux — *A Chocolate-Coated Savoy Cake*
Bourdelots — *Pastry-Covered Apples or Pears*
Chausson — *Apple Turnovers*
Buckwheat Crepes

BRITTANY
The Breton Sardine
Fish (Conger Eel) Soup
Grilled or Broiled Tuna

Breton Sole
Lobster and Spiny Lobster
Shrimp
Mussels, Cockles, Clams, and Petoncles
Scallops
Breton Andouille *Sausages*
Poultry Stuffing for Fat Birds
Breton Leg of Lamb
Buckwheat Crepes
Le Lait Ribaud — *Laughing Milk*
More Desserts

BURGUNDY, LYONNAISE REGION
Braised Leg of Lamb with Onions
Stuffed Calf Ears
Steamed Truffled Bresse Hen
Chicken Fricassee — with Onions, Thyme, and Cream
Celestine's Chicken
The Meat Pies of Bugey
Crawfish Nantua Style
The Fondue of Belley
The Black Morels of Valromey

FRANCHE-COMTÉ
Panade
Frog Legs Stock
Les Gaudes — *Polenta*
Macaroni Timbale
Quenelles — *Pike Forcemeat*
The True Woodcock Salmis — *Stew*
Potée — *Bacon and Vegetable Soup*
Matefaim *or* Matafam — *Sweet Fritters*
Fromagerè

ALSACE

Choucroute
Ham, Baked in Crust
Bakenofe — *A Casserole of Pork and Lamb, Onion, and Potato*
Onion Tart
Tarte au Fromage Blanc — *White Cheese Tart*
Red Cabbage
Kafferkrautz — *Twisted Crown*
Kougelhopf — *Almond Yeast Cake*

LORRAINE

Foie Gras — *Goose or Duck Liver Terrine*
Lorraine Meat Pie
Quiche Lorraine
Game Terrine
Lorraine Noodles
Ramekin — *A Cheese Soufflé*
Lorraine Crepes
Knepfen *or* Kneppes — *Gnocchi*
Matelote de *Metz* — *A Fish Stew Made with Red Wine*
Financière *Cake from Nancy* — *A Veal Soufflé*
Lost Rice or Rice Pudding
Kougelhopf — *Yeast Cake with Raisins*
Plombière — *Amaretti Soufflé*
Chocolate Cake

SAVOY AND DAUPHINE

Trout Meunière
Le Gratin Dauphinois — *Baked Scalloped Potatoes*
Matefaim — *A Large Buckwheat Pancake*

LIMOUSIN

Gâteau Limousin — Clafoutis — *Cherries Baked in Batter*
Las Farsaduras *(also known as* Farcidure*)* — *Cabbage Soup with
Stuffed Cabbage Leaves*
Stuffed Mushrooms and Potatoes
Lou Cassa-Musel — *Limousin Cake*

AUVERGNE

Cabbage Soup
Celeriac (Celery Root) Soup
Leg of Lamb with Potatoes
Rouchides — *Potatoes with Bacon*
Lamb Salmis — *Lamb Cooked with Red Wine*
Coq au Vin — *Chicken Braised in Red Wine*
Boudins — *Sausages with Apples*
Mushrooms
La Tarte au Papa — *Papa's Tart*
Le Cadet Mathieu — *An Apple Pie*
Acacia Fritters
Cheeses

AVEYRON

Petites — *"Little Ones"* — *Stuffed Tripe Packages*
Foie Gras au Gratin — *Casseroled Goose or Duck Liver*
Chicken Fricassee Villefranche Style — *with Ham and Onions*
Shoulder of Lamb with Pistachios
Hare en Cabessal
Oulade — *A Vegetable Soup*
Mourtayrol — Pot-au-Feu *with Beef, Chicken, and Ham*
Confits d'Oies — *Preserved Goose*

PROVENCE

Aigo-Boulido — *A Soup Made with Boiled Water and Olive Oil*
Chickpea Soup and Chickpea Salad
Bouillabaisse — *A Fish Soup*
Aioli — *Garlic-Flavored Mayonnaise*
Bourride — *A Fish Soup*
Poutargue des Martigues — *Caviar Made with Mullet Roe*
Red Mullets Niçoise
Mussels with Spinach
Eggplant Provençale
Artichokes Provençale
Small Birds
Stuffed Sardines

LANGUEDOC

Preserved or Fresh Cèpes Nîmoise
Stuffed Tomatoes —With Meat or Bread Crumb Stuffing
Snails Nîmoise
Lamb Carbonnade

BÉARN

Garbure — *Cabbage Soup*
Bouillie — *To Be Served with* Garbure
Les Confits Béarnaise — *Preserved Goose or Duck*
Piperade — *A Tomato Sauce to Pour Over Fried Eggs*

GASCONY AND THE BORDELAISE REGION

Daube
Grape Harvester's Soup
Tourin Bordelais e — *Onion Soup*
Landais Omelet
Bouchées Pauillacaises — *Potato Balls with Meat Filling*
Manchons de Boeuf — *Beef Bundles Filled with* Cèpes

Game Surprises From Périgueux
Hare Sauce from Orignac
Grape Harvester's Turkey Wings
Veal Fanchette
Sautéed Chicken Bordelaise
Cèpes *(Porcini)* Bordelaise
Eggplant Bordelaise
Cassoulet de Castelnaudary
Lombézien *Cake — A Pistachio Charlotte*
Bavarois aux Marrons *— A Chestnut Cream*

DRINKS
Coffee
Tea
Chamomile
Hot Lemonade
Poule *(Chicken) Milk*

French Flanders

The child of the north, the child of Flanders— *le P'tit Quin-quin,* as they call him— is certainly not a spoiled child. He is reared under a somber sky and surrounded by a somber landscape. Smoke and coal dust from the factory chimneys blacken his town like a veil.

So it comes as no surprise that he is not a very demanding gourmand. A slice of spiced bread or a little jar of walnuts preserved in molasses will be enough to gladden his heart for a long time and keep him going in his daily life. Later, when he has become the solid yet passionate Flemish realist, known throughout history as someone who fights for his ideas, he will not search out food that is the least bit complicated or has any finesse. He prefers quantity rather than quality. Generous family dinners, beer, and good liqueurs are all he wants. He needs food to warm him in the fight against the fog and cold, food to bring sunshine to his heart.

The reason he doesn't ordinarily drink wine is because his country does not produce it, and therefore it is expensive to buy. But when the Flamand can afford it, he is certainly not amateurish about wine, but a real connoisseur, particularly of Burgundies. He can drink a huge amount without losing his *sang-froid.*

Because of these peculiarities, I am somewhat embarrassed when talking about Flemish specialties. Those who know, say, "There are hardly any, except boiled beef, poached chicken with white sauce, smoked bacon, sausages with cabbage, tripe, and rabbit cooked with *eau-de-vie,* grapes, and prunes. These dishes are the core of Flemish cooking." The principal desserts are: a red plum tart with luscious pastry; *les oublies* [small, cylindrical or horn-shaped waffles]; *les couques au beurre* [buttery sugary cake-like tarts]; *pain d'épices* [spiced cake]; *les coeurs d'Arras* [gingerbread]; *les Condés d'Amiens* [almond puff-pastry cake]; *gaufrettes* [thin wafers]; and waffles. Let me also mention *moines* [friars], which are pears or apples wrapped in a thick pastry. They are baked in the baker's oven with sugar and water in the bottom of the dish, which creates a little caramel.

All these dishes are rather simple dishes, even basic. Some Flemish just eat pickled roll-mop herrings with a glass of beer. This is supposed to be good for you! Oven-baked potatoes with lots of cheese and butter are equally well loved. On every street corner, vendors of french fries are very successful, as are vendors of steamed potatoes, with their small carts, who cook their vegetables in a curious huge pot that has kept the same shape probably for centuries.

Beer is the most popular drink in Flanders. There are both dark and light beers that have good heads of foam and are, of course, very high in alcohol. Near Cassel or Hazebrouck they also drink mead (a mild drink made from honey). Gin from Wambrechies, near Lille, appeals not only to the Flemish but has succeeded in acquiring a worldwide reputation. *Boulisse,* a drink made from warmed wine mixed with sugar and *eau-de-vie,* is an excellent nightcap for colds.

It is somewhat unneccesary to add that in the rich industrial areas there are diverse food styles, as there are elsewhere, and that this diversity, combined with wealth, makes for a grand Flemish dinner—though it would be only a snack for Pantagruel [a Rabelais character, a glutton].

This is the only country where I have seen huge asparagus tips served like asparagus spears, that is to say, just the heads, without the stems, dressed with a *mousseline* sauce, served in a vegetable dish.

Recipes from the provinces of Artois and the Somme do not differ much from those of Flanders.

Here are two excellent Flemish recipes that were given to me. They are unusual and well researched.

Sauce for Roast Hare

This thick, dark, excellent sauce accompanies roast hare admirably.

- 4 onions, chopped
- 6 peppercorns
- 1 pinch nutmeg
- 2 cloves
- 1 bay leaf
- 3 tablespoons unsalted butter
  Liver and heart of the hare, chopped
- ¼ cup vinegar
- 2 cups red wine
- 1 teaspoon sugar
- 1 tablespoon potato flour or cornstarch

Sauté the onions, peppercorns, nutmeg, cloves, and a bay leaf in butter in a saucepan. Add the liver and heart of the hare and moisten with vinegar.

Simmer for 1 hour, keeping an eye on it and stirring every now and again. If you think it will dry out, add some boiling water and more vinegar, so as to retain the taste of vinegar.

At the end of an hour, rub the sauce through a fine sieve. Add the red wine and sugar and put back on the fire to bring to a boil and simmer for another 20 minutes. Bind the sauce with potato flour (see *roux* in the Glossary, page 263).

Yield: 1½ cups.

Thrush

4   ounces (1 stick) unsalted butter
8   thrush [or quail]
6   juniper berries for each bird, crushed

Melt the butter in a saucepan over a low fire. Brown the thrush all over in the butter. Cover the saucepan.

After 20 minutes, when the thrush are halfway cooked, add the crushed juniper berries.

Finish the cooking and serve the thrush hot.

Serves 4.

Ile de France

Paris is the city where you can find the very best produce, if you really want to and know how. Paris imports the most beautiful fruits, vegetables, fish, and poultry from all over France. However, Paris leaves something to be desired on two essential points: meat and milk.

A good Parisian butcher is rare; it depends on the district of Paris where you live. The established rule seems to be that the best of them serve you badly one out of three times. Maybe they just can't help themselves. Doubtless this is why in even the most expensive restaurants (I haven't said the best) meats are always covered with sauce, masked with aspic, or concealed by over-seasoning. *Chiquettes, tournedos, noisettes,* or *filets mignons* are offered in restaurants with a variety of accompaniments. In my opinion, large pieces of meat are always of better quality than small.

I will not be so bold as to list here the specialties of each Parisian restaurant. I will content myself by giving to all true gourmands who like eating at home, and for whom I have written this little book, the advice to try and get their meat from Touraine, where it is exquisite. All you need to do is order once or twice a week from Rocheteau, butcher at Mosnes (Indre et Loire). You will have the pleasure of eating firm white veal and fresh plump kidneys. A rib of beef is a rich red; the fat is as good as the lean. Juices spurt out when you cut into it. A young lamb, who has certainly gamboled in the fields, is still tender and full of flavor. Thick slices of calf's liver stay pink and tender when cooked—whereas in Paris they are often dry, gray, and tough like the old soles of a poor man's shoes.

Good milk is even more difficult to obtain. I have tried them all, from large dairies to the local milkmen—they are all the same, even those that are expensive and have been specially tested by doctors. They are too rich, too yellow, too buttery, too artificial. All of them, even those that cost 1 franc 75 centimes per liter, taste slightly off in a cup of *café au lait*. I think it is impossible to find good milk in Paris because it has to pass through too many hands before it gets to us. I am resigned to the fact, that's all.

Apart from these problems, you can buy the finest produce in the best condition if you go to the trouble to visit Les Halles early in the morning. Or at least go to markets where you can *choose* your own. One of the worst faults of good cooks is that they become distracted in the market; when they chat too much, they end up with second-quality produce.

What is the character of Parisian cooking? Is there one? Although I am Parisian and I adore Paris, I reply without hesitation that its food is most often cooked by people in a hurry. It is not made with tender loving care, so it is not very good. What they call lunch in Paris usually consists of two fried eggs, followed by a chop with fried potatoes and then a green vegetable.

But what french fries! There is nowhere else, except in Paris, where they are so crisp, so light, and so delicious. Whether they are sliced as thin as paper or cut in thin matchsticks, the potatoes are excellent. They are good no matter how they are cut. But you have to have that special touch, and a little inspiration, in order to cook them.

French Fries

Here is my advice: Peel the potatoes with a knife that does not smell of garlic. Slice each potato into very thin rounds or into very thin little sticks. Throw them into cold water. Strain and dry them, then cook them in at least 2 inches of hot oil [375 degrees] that is singing on a brisk fire. Don't cook too many at a time, because each piece of potato must cook separately. When they are crisp and golden, remove them from the fat with a skimmer, place them on a platter, and keep them warm in a hot 400-degree oven. Sprinkle them with fine salt to taste.

If you see them become soft or soggy, put them in the hot oil a second time. Keep the temperature of the oil constant and cook them quickly, gaily, and with a light hand.

This is not a foolproof recipe—there are some cooks who never succeed, and I don't know why.

To tell the truth, apart from these sublime potatoes, everyone knows that you can eat much better in other regions, where all good old traditions still exist. In Paris, modern cooking schools make a mess of their cooks. They teach them to make small Chinese dishes with long complicated garnishes that turn cold as you make them. They totally neglect the fundamental principles of cooking.

For all that, I will give recipes for *Petits Pois Parisienne* [Peas] and *Langouste Parisienne* [Spiny Lobster], which are two very celebrated dishes from our city.

Petits Pois Parisienne

2½ cups fresh shelled peas or 12 ounces frozen peas
1 cup water
¼ head Boston lettuce, shredded
1 onion, finely chopped
1 tablespoon unsalted butter
   Salt and freshly ground black pepper
1 teaspoon sugar

Boil water in a saucepan and add peas, lettuce, and onions, cooking 10 to 15 minutes for fresh peas, 5 minutes for frozen peas. When they are cooked, drain them and put them back into the saucepan. Add the butter, salt and pepper, and sugar. Serve immediately.

Serves 4.

Langouste Parisienne

The worst attempt at refinement would be to slice the lobster's tail meat and serve it arranged on a pedestal, like a phantom ship — especially as the lobster loses flavor when it is sliced too thinly.

    1 nice lively 1½-pound lobster
      Cold water
    2 lettuce hearts
      Mayonnaise
    2 large hard-boiled eggs

Bring a pot of water to the boil. Grab the lobster by its body and submerge it in the boiling water. Cook for 15 minutes from the time you put it in the water. When it is cooked, take it out of the water with tongs and chill down by running cold water over it for a few minutes.

[Split the lobster from head to tail with a knife. Slice the tail meat in ¾-inch slices. Crack the claws with the aid of a hammer, nut or lobster crackers.]

Serve the lobster in its shell with a garnish of lettuce hearts coated with mayonnaise and halves of hard-boiled eggs.

In a sauceboat, serve a light mayonnaise [mixed with the red cooked roe, only available if the lobster is female].

Serves 1 or 2.

Lobster Bourg-la-Reine

This recipe is a near replica of the well-known Lobster *à l'Americaine*. [Bourg-la-Reine is on the outskirts of Paris, where the Daudet family used to live.] Serve this delicious lobster with rice *à l'Indienne* (recipe follows). There is nothing better than this dish.
    Start this recipe the day before it's to be eaten.

    1 *court-bouillon* (see Glossary, page 260) with lots of
      onions and carrots
    1 *bouquet garni* (see Glossary, page 259)

20 peppercorns
    Pinch cayenne pepper
    Water
 2 1½-pound lobsters
 3 pounds tomatoes, peeled, seeded, and chopped
 5 cloves garlic, minced
    Salt and freshly ground black pepper
 4 sprigs fresh thyme
 1 bay leaf
 3 medium-size onions, chopped
 2 tablespoons unsalted butter
 2 tablespoons all-purpose flour
 ¼ cup cognac
 1 whole garlic clove, crushed

Make a *court-bouillon* with the *bouquet garni,* peppercorns, and cayenne pepper and water in a large pot. Bring it to a boil. Add the lobsters and cook for 7 minutes from the time you put them in the *court-bouillon.*

Place the chopped tomatoes in a saucepan with garlic, salt, pepper, thyme, bay leaf, and onions. Cook for 20 minutes over moderate heat.

Melt the butter in a large casserole over moderate heat and stir in the flour. Push the tomato mixture through a food mill into the butter and flour. Stir well so it does not get lumpy—the sauce must be smooth.

Add cognac and garlic. Cut the lobster in pieces and add to the sauce. Simmer gently for 7 minutes.

Refrigerate the lobster and sauce in a dish or bowl overnight.

Reheat the dish carefully before serving. Remove the garlic if you want.

Serves 4.

Rice à l'Indienne

3   quarts water
1   tablespoon salt
2   cups rice

Bring the water to a boil in a pot. Throw in the salt and rice and let boil gently for 17 minutes. Some types of rice take only 15 minutes to cook.

When the rice is cooked, drain it well in a colander.

Form a beautiful snowy mountain of rice in a deep dish. Each grain must have its own personality, and it should not resemble that awful pap when rice is overcooked and even a cat would not deign to eat it.

Serves 4.

Veal Terrine Armenonville

6   1½-inch-thick pieces of veal shank (3 to 3½ pounds)
    [otherwise known as *osso bucco*] — detach
    the meat from the bones (save the bones) and remove
    the thin skin and fat
2   tablespoons unsalted butter
4   medium-size onions, halved
4   carrots, peeled and cut in chunks
1   cup strong veal stock
1   *bouquet garni* (see Glossary, page 259)
1   teaspoon *quatre épices* (see Glossary, page 263)
    Salt and freshly ground black pepper
3   sprigs flat-leaf parsley

Preheat the oven to 350 degrees. Place the veal and bones, butter, onions, carrots, and veal stock in a heavy covered casserole. Bake for 1 hour, remove from the oven, and let stand ½ hour. Discard the bones.

Extract the meat from the casserole and shred with two forks (as when making *rillettes*) or mash the meat on a chopping board with a fork. You may use the food processor, but the mixture has a better texture when shredded by hand.

[Place a dozen flat-leaf parsley leaves in the bottom of a loaf pan or terrine 5 inches by 8½ inches, and 3 inches deep.] Pile the shredded meat on top of the parsley, and fill to the top with hot, well-seasoned, finely strained and degreased stock from the casserole. Chill and serve with the onions and carrots, if you wish.

Serves 8.

Chicken Franchard

You can enjoy this dish at Franchard, in the middle of the Fontainebleau forests, at the Ermitage Restaurant. In this charming and poetic place, it takes on a unique flavor and leaves you with delicious memories. However, you don't have to eat Chicken Franchard in a forest. You can make and serve this dish just as successfully in a fourth-floor apartment, on the most bourgeois table, even one made of mahogany.

- 1   3½- to 4-pound chicken, cut in 9 pieces, (see Glossary, page 260)
- 3   tablespoons unsalted butter
- 1   tablespoon each chervil, parsley, and thyme, finely chopped
- 2   tablespoons tarragon, finely chopped

1   clove garlic, minced
     Salt and freshly ground black pepper
¼   pound mushrooms, chopped or sliced
2   tablespoons all-purpose flour
1½ cups rich chicken stock
8   triangles of bread fried in butter (croutons)

Brown the chicken pieces with the butter in a casserole.

Add the herbs, garlic, salt and pepper.

Add the mushrooms and then sprinkle with the flour, mixing it in thoroughly so it doesn't lump. Add the stock.

Cover and simmer for 20 minutes or until chicken is tender. The sauce should be thick and golden in color.

If you want to reduce the sauce, to make it thicker, put the chicken pieces and mushrooms in a serving dish in a warm place, and cook until the sauce is to your liking. Pour the sauce over the chicken and garnish with fried bread.

Serves 4.

Veal Scallops Franchard

Veal Scallops Franchard is cooked in exactly the same way as Chicken Franchard (see above), except that you will sauté the scallops. It's a good idea to add 2 tomatoes—cook them separately and rub them through a sieve into the sauce, after you add the stock. Reduce the sauce by further cooking. It will liven up the veal.

Fried Gudgeons

Fried gudgeons are worth eating only in a tiny bar by the side of the Seine, washed down with a slightly dry Chablis *ordinaire*. Accompany the fish with buttered bread.

   1   cup all-purpose flour
   ½   teaspoon freshly ground black pepper
   ¼   teaspoon cayenne pepper
   1½ pounds gudgeon [or smelt, whitebait, or silversides]
       Deep-frying vegetable oil
   4   lemon wedges
   1   tablespoon salt

Mix the flour with black pepper and cayenne pepper. Roll a few fish at a time in the seasoned flour and fry in 2 inches oil at 375 degrees.

Fry until crisp. Keep warm in a 200-degree oven.

Serve with lemon wedges.

The fish must be fried until crisp. Salt them only after they have been cooked.

Serves 4.

La Matelote —*Freshwater Fish Stew*

In order for this *bouillabaisse* of the north to have just the right taste and charm, it must be eaten beside the Seine. *Matelote* is a landscape unto itself. It immediately evokes a deep, fast flowing river, a gray and stormy sky, a blurred, undefined horizon, water lapping against stone steps, the grating of a chain holding a boat against the river bank, the straight lines of a tow path, large tufts of reeds surrounding little islands, and a tangle of weeds and glistening grasses bending and turning in the water. You idly watch the sudden appearance of a stump of dead wood, an old hat, or a float, without dreaming of anything, lost in a special reverie beside the river's edge.

Matelote has all that, and when you carry it hot and steaming to the table in its large, deep, heavy, white porcelain dish — with its pyramid of fried croutons, quarters of hard-cooked eggs, and different shapes of fish — if the landscape that I have just talked about does not enter with the dish, it won't be any good — not worth a single taste. All other stylish or sophisticated *matelotes*, made with white wine, made with old wine, garnished with crayfish or mushrooms, are not worth any more than this simple *matelote* from the river bed. Good cooks know this only too well.

1	3-pound carp, whitefish, or pike, or 2½ pounds fillets
1	eel
	All-purpose flour for rolling fish slices
4	tablespoons unsalted butter
1	pound pearl onions, peeled (see Glossary, page 263)
2	tablespoons all-purpose flour
1	cup water
2	cups red wine
	Salt and freshly ground black pepper
1	*bouquet garni* (see Glossary, page 259)
1	clove garlic, crushed
½	cup cognac
8	slices toasted bread
8	large hard-boiled eggs

Rinse the fish. Scale it, gut it, cut off the fins, and slice it. Get rid of the head because it looks terrible.

The eel can be skinned or not. It can be cooked with the skin on in this dish, and it will be extremely good, if a little oily. Remove the head of the eel also, because it looks like a snake's head. Roll the slices of fish in plenty of flour.

In a large shallow earthenware casserole or frying pan, brown the pieces of fish in the butter, over moderate heat. Put aside and then fry the onions in the same butter. Add 2 tablespoons flour and blend in the water. Stir with a wooden spoon and check to see that the *roux* (see Glossary, page 263) does not become too thick. Add the red wine, salt and pepper, and the *bouquet garni* with garlic.

When the onions have cooked for 20 minutes, throw in the pieces of fish. 5 minutes later, add the cognac and flame it as you would a punch.

Cook for another 5 minutes or so. The sauce must be a little thick, but not too thick.

Don't forget to remove the *bouquet garni* and garlic before serving.

Serve on slices of toasted bread and add hard-boiled eggs, quartered.

Serves 8.

Entrecôte *Bercy* — *Grilled Beef Steak*

This is also a dish from the boatmen that asks to be eaten outdoors.

> 2 6- to 10-ounce pieces of sirloin steak, neither too thin nor too small (one piece per person)
> Salt and freshly ground black pepper

6 tablespoons unsalted butter, softened
2 teaspoons each parsley and chervil, finely chopped
2 shallots, minced

Sprinkle both sides of the steak with salt and pepper. Grill over a hot fire. While it is cooking, mix—over very low fire in a small pan, with a fork—the butter with the chopped herbs, and shallot, until creamy.

Just before serving, place half the butter on two hot serving plates. Place the cooked steaks on top and the rest of the butter on the top of the steaks.

Serve very hot.

Serves 2.

Fried Entrecôte *Bercy*

4 tablespoons unsalted butter
2 6- to 10-ounce sirloin steaks
4 tablespoons vinegar
2 teaspoons each parsley, chervil, and chives,
finely chopped
Salt and freshly ground black pepper

Melt the butter in a frying pan. When it is very hot, add the steaks and let them cook, turning over now and again with a fork.

When they are cooked to your liking, remove them and put on a hot plate in a warm place or cover with a lid.

Pour the vinegar into the pan and add the chopped herbs; swirl them around in the pan and pour over the steaks.

Serve at once.

Serves 2.

Rich Macaroni

In general, the French do not really know how to deal with pasta. Most often the noodles and macaroni served to us are only considered fit for Friday (fasting-day) meals. They are usually dull and wan, badly overcooked, and taste of dirty linen. However, a well-cooked macaroni dish can be a real treat. Here is a recipe that is worth making.

1½ pounds onions, cut in 8 wedges each
¼ pound (1 stick) unsalted butter
    Salt and freshly ground black pepper
4 pounds beef top round, rump, or boneless chuck, in 1 piece
4 pounds tomatoes, roughly chopped
2 pounds medium-size macaroni
6 ounces grated Parmesan cheese

Brown the onions in the butter in a heavy casserole. Sprinkle salt and pepper on the beef and when the onions are browned, move them to the side and brown the meat on all sides. Cover and simmer, turning the meat over every hour for 3½ to 4 hours.

Simmer the tomatoes in a separate saucepan with salt and pepper, but no water. After ½ hour, when they are tender, rub them through a sieve or strainer.

Preheat the oven to 400 degrees.

Bring a large pot of salted water to a boil, throw in the macaroni, and cook according to package directions. When it is cooked, strain well to get rid of all the moisture. Mix the tomato sauce with the *jus* from the meat.

In a deep casserole or a wide earthenware casserole, place a layer of macaroni, topped by grated Parmesan, a layer of sauce, a layer of macaroni, and so on. Bake for 30 minutes.

This dish is exquisite. [Eat the meat on another occasion. It is excellent served chilled.]

Serves 8 to 10.

Crepes Mollettes — *Soft Delicate Crepes*

This is the way to obtain soft delicate crepes. [You can find orange-flower water at health food stores or pharmacies.]

- 10 ounces (2⅛ cups) all-purpose flour
- 4 large eggs, yolks and whites separated
- 2 cups milk
- 1 cup sugar
- ½ cup mineral water
- 2 tablespoons orange-flower water

[Mix the batter in a blender or] whisk the wet ingredients slowly into the dry, so there are no lumps. Add the egg yolks one by one, stirring and beating well. Let this semi-fluid batter rest for 2 hours.

Beat the egg whites until stiff and fold into the batter just before cooking the crepes.

Pour ½ cup batter into a lightly buttered frying pan over moderate heat. Tilt the pan so the batter spreads out 6 inches in diameter. Cook for 1 minute, and when bubbles appear on the surface, turn the crepe over and cook another minute. Adjust the fire under the pan if the crepes become too dark in color.

For each crepe you will need to add a little butter to the pan.

Yield: 16 crepes.

Leon Daudet's Crepes

[These crepes are savory.]

1 recipe Crepes *Mollettes*. Do not add sugar or orange-
flower water.

Filling

2 cups chopped boiled beef from a *pot-au-feu*
(see page 14)

2 tablespoons each parsley and chervil, or tarragon,
finely chopped

3 tablespoons melted butter
Salt and freshly ground black pepper

Preheat the oven to 350 degrees.

Mix the beef, parsley, chervil, and butter together with salt and
pepper.

Roll the filling inside each crepe and bake for 15 minutes. Serve
very hot.

A bit filling, but excellent.

Yield: 16 crepes.

Touraine

One way to overlook Touraine is to dash through it superficially. You might be one of those wild travelers who, in a cloud of dust, only drives along the banks of the Loire between Blois and Tours. Perhaps you think you can take in the horizon, the trees, the villages, and all the charms of the river in one quick glance.

On the contrary: you have to live in Touraine so you can examine it at your leisure and learn to understand and love it. You must walk in the plains, under a splendid blue sky, in the gold and silver fields of wheat and oats, and follow the slopes where rows of vines seem like armies on the march. You must stop in the road and feel the heat. You will feel blessed when your eyes alight on a lark, drunk with joy, who pierces the blue sky with a song that reaches insane heights. You must walk in the valleys and take the sheltered lanes that lead to the forest. You must go into the villages and kneel on a wooden pew in a cool, echoing church.

You must also pass through the door of an inn, enter a large, whitewashed room where exposed beams are set into the ceiling, and sit down near the window at a table covered with a slightly sticky oil cloth, on which flies sleep. Ask for bread, a fresh chèvre cheese, and a good bottle of local wine (perhaps you want a bottle of fizzy lemonade also). You must be served by a very old hag with a pointed chin who has her spectacles perched on her forehead.

Finally, you must experience a whole day of great heat, refresh yourself by the light of the moon, and cross through a sleeping village beside a plain that is so calm and beautiful it seems it will endure forever.

Then you will know Touraine and can appreciate its products.

The *charcuterie* [pork store] in Touraine is especially recommended. Without dismissing the universally appreciated and
well-known *rillettes de Tours* [potted shredded pork], I must
mention the *andouille de Tours* [sausages made with pig en-
trails], which are so fat and moist. But these are not the only
good sausages, for there are excellent ones in Blois, Amboise,
and usually in all the small towns of Touraine. The large *rillettes
de ménage*, in which you find here and there a small piece of
pork, make a refreshing change from all that fat. Even more
charming are the *rillons* [potted cubes of pork] which, although
kept chilled, are even more delightful when slightly warmed in
the oven. *Rillons* are made with the leftovers of a pig from
which they have taken the hams, made the *boudins* [blood
sausages], cut up the ribs, tied the roasts, cut off the feet, prepared the brawn, and so on. They collect all the small leftover
pieces and cook them in butter until golden. The *rillons* are
then chilled.

The meats of Touraine, such as veal, beef, and lamb are
equally succulent. I have already mentioned this in the intro-
duction to the Ile de France, and I repeat it here. The only in-
convenience is that the meat in the villages is sometimes too
fresh, and therefore a little tough. In the towns this is not as
likely to happen, and if you know how to choose good meat
you will do well.

Why is the meat so especially good in Touraine? It is because the animals pass their time on the fields or banks of the
Loire. These countless pastures, filled with a thousand different
perfumed herbs, empart something ephemeral to their flesh.

There is something strange in the fact that the people of
Touraine do not make good butter. The peasants don't know
how to make it and haven't bothered to learn. I have often no-
ticed that the cows are badly kept and are caked with manure.
It would be a great source of income if they established model
farms where one could obtain butter that does not go rancid
right away, and good creamy cheeses as well.

Now let's talk about vegetables. They grow easily when watered properly. The soil of Touraine swells them up with a delicate sap. The best *petits pois,* fava beans, and *haricots verts* that I have ever eaten in my life were those of Touraine; they cook them in a special way.

Fava Beans Tourangelle

You can prepare *haricots verts* or *petits pois* in the same way.

Peas do not need parsley or chervil, just a little savory or a lettuce that is cooked down in its juices at the same time as the peas.

> 2   pounds beautiful green fava beans (this becomes
>   2 cups when shelled)
>   Cold water
>   Salt
> 3   sprigs savory
> 2   sprigs parsley
> 1   large egg yolk
> 1   tablespoon unsalted butter
> 1   teaspoon each parsley, chervil, and savory,
>   finely chopped

Split the fava beans open with your fingernail, one by one, and remove the thick furry pod that covers them and is inedible. Cook them in a pan of lightly salted water over moderate heat with sprigs of savory and parsley.

After 5 to 6 minutes, when they are cooked, strain them off, saving ½ cup cooking water. As a refinement, peel off the grayish skin from the fava beans when they are cool enough to handle. Return them to another saucepan with the butter and heat over a low fire. Stir the egg yolk into the reserved water and bring to a simmer. Stir with a wooden spoon until you see the sauce just begin to thicken. Add to the beans and add salt to taste if necessary. Take off the fire immediately and serve in a deep platter, adding the finely chopped "requisites" — the parsley, chervil, and savory.

Serves 4.

Green Walnuts

These green walnuts are wonderful when well made. You must prepare them at the end of September, when the leaves begin to yellow and crackle. They have the flavor of autumn and stimulate the appetite. If you cannot obtain *verjus,* use a little vinegar diluted with water—however, it won't be as good. [You can gather green walnuts in September through November off trees. They have a soft round green covering around a very hard black shell. They are also called black walnuts. You will need a nutcracker designed to handle black walnuts or a hammer to open them. See Sources on page 266. Also see Sources for shelled black walnuts.]

>   12 green walnuts or very fresh walnuts
>   1½ cups *verjus* (see Glossary, page 264)
>   1 teaspoon freshly ground black pepper
>   1 shallot, minced

Shell the walnuts and pick them over (there must be no bitter skin remaining on them). In autumn the walnuts are very tender, and their flesh is milky.

Break them in two and place them in a deep plate filled halfway with *verjus* (see Glossary, page 264). Sprinkle with pepper, add the minced shallot, and marinate for about 1 hour. Before serving, strain off the shallots and place the nuts and *verjus* in an hors d'oeuvre dish.

Serves 3 as an appetizer.

Orleans

Grilled Herring

Many peasants in the center of France, especially in the Orleans region, enjoy these herrings.

> 1 beautiful gold herring weighing ½ pound, split for you by the fishmonger
> Vinaigrette (see page 57), made with lots of pepper
> 1 teaspoon chopped *fines herbes* (see Glossary, page 261)
> 1 shallot, minced

Lie the herring flat on the grill. Grill both sides.

Add finely chopped *fines herbes* and minced shallot to the vinaigrette.

Serve the herring hot. Eat it with the vinaigrette.

Go to bed without speaking to a single person.

Serves 1.

Jellied Carp

Prepare the carp the morning of or the day before needed, to give it time to jell.

> 1 3 pound carp [whitefish, pike, or bass], scaled and gutted, with fins and head cut off, sliced into 5 slices or 2½ pounds fillets

3   onions, roughly chopped
1   clove garlic
1   tablespoon parsley, chopped
    Salt and freshly ground black pepper
1   cup dry white wine or cold water
1   pound small button mushrooms, brushed clean
2   tablespoons all-purpose flour
2   tablespoons olive oil
¼   pound small cooked shrimp

Place the slices of fish in a pan with onions, garlic, parsley, salt and pepper, wine or water, mushrooms, flour, and olive oil. This marinade must cover the fish.

Bring to a boil, uncovered, and continue to cook gently for 20 minutes.

When the fish is cooked, take the pieces out of the pan and arrange them in a shallow casserole. Place the mushrooms around them and pour the sauce through a sieve over the top. The sauce jells as it cools. Refrigerate.

Decorate the casserole with beautiful pink shrimp.

Serves 5.

Hare à la Royale

I believe there are several recipes for Hare *à la Royale.* Here is one (perhaps not the original recipe) that gives good results.

1   beautiful skinned and gutted hare (from Beauce) [or a rabbit, weighing 3 to 4 pounds]

Stuffing

- 2 cups fresh bread crumbs
- ¾ cup chicken stock
- 1½ cups finely chopped bacon
- 3 tablespoons parsley, finely chopped
  Salt and freshly ground black pepper
- 2 large egg yolks
- 1 black truffle, minced [or 1 tablespoon black truffle puree (Salsa Tartufata by Urbani, see Sources, page 265), or 1 teaspoon white truffle oil]
- 1 large thin sheet of pork fat, available from the butcher
- 2 carrots, peeled and sliced
- 1 onion, quartered
- 1 bay leaf
- 3 sprigs fresh thyme
  Freshly ground black pepper
  a pinch *quatre épices* (see Glossary, page 263)
- 1 tablespoon cornstarch dissolved in 2 tablespoons cold water
- 2 tablespoons vinegar
  Salt and freshly ground black pepper

Make a stuffing with bread crumbs soaked in stock. Add the bacon, parsley, salt, pepper, egg yolks, and minced truffle. Fill the body of the hare with it.

Sew up the opening. Wrap the body of the hare with a large thin sheet of pork fat. Shape the body into a round, head to tail, tying the four feet together.

Preheat the oven to 400 degrees.

Place the hare in a roasting pan with carrots, onion, bay leaf, thyme, pepper, and *quatre épices.*

Roast a hare for 3 hours, or 1½ hours for a rabbit. Place the hare on a platter and cover with foil to keep warm. Mix the cornstarch and water with vinegar and salt and pepper in a saucepan.

Degrease the sauce from the roasting pan and add to the mixture in the saucepan. Before serving, place the sauce on moderate heat and cook gently until it has thickened. Pour over the meat.

You need not carve the meat, just serve it with spoons.

Serves 4 to 6.

Perche

Tripe à la Mode d'Authon du Perche

3   pounds tripe, sliced in 1½-inch slices
1   pound pork belly, sliced in 1½-inch slices
1   bunch carrots, peeled and sliced
3   large onions, roughly chopped
1   bunch thyme
3   bay leaves
6   parsley sprigs
    Salt and freshly ground black pepper
⅔   cup cognac
    Parchment paper or aluminum foil

Preheat the oven to 300 degrees.

Place layers of pork belly, tripe, carrots, and onions in a deep, oven-proof pot. Top the layers with thyme, bay leaves, and parsley. Sprinkle lightly with salt and pepper. Finally, pour over the cognac.

Cover with parchment paper and a lid, to seal it hermetically. Bake for 3 hours.

Serves 8.

Poitou

Poitou does not offer much culinary variety. The countryside itself has no distinctive characteristics — the valleys are too narrow, the horizons too limited. It is as if young Clain had tied together with his silver ribbon a whole collection of beautiful paintings or chromos (chromolithographs) that are cheerful, banal, and totally forgettable.

However, this does not prevent the Poitevins from being charming people and genuine gourmands. They are aware of the lack of resources in their region and know how to take advantage of their proximity to Anjou and Touraine to obtain delicious wines. They also know how to prepare all the excellent dishes of France with care.

So, of the local recipes, I will only give Cheese *Tourte*. *Clafoutis Poitevin* is just like *Clafoutis Limousin* (see page 183). Let me also mention the little *aiguillettes* (duck breasts, or sometimes just the tenderloin from the breast) that are grilled outside during village festivals, and the vulgar *galettes*, called *fouaces* (butter rolls). The real speciality of Poitou is a small cheese made with goat's milk that they call *chabichou*.

Cheese Tourte

1   recipe *pâté brisée* (see Glossary, *pâté brisée* I, page 262)
1   11-ounce log of goat cheese (*chèvre*)
6   large eggs, separated
    Pinch salt
½   cup sugar

½ cup *crème fraîche* (see Glossary, page 260)
3 tablespoons cornstarch
1 teaspoon cognac or orange-flower water

Preheat the oven to 400 degrees.

Line a metal bowl 9 inches in diameter and 3 inches deep with the *pâté brisée*. Press heavy duty aluminum foil onto the raw pastry and bake for 15 minutes, uncovering the pastry in the last 5 minutes. Do not turn off the oven.

Beat together all the ingredients except the egg whites until smooth. Beat the egg whites separately until stiff. Fold them into the cheese mixture and pour into the baked pastry.

Bake for 45 to 50 minutes until mixture is firm and the top quite dark. When cool enough to handle, unmold and cut in wedges.

Serves 6 to 8.

Champagne

Turkey or Chicken Champenois

1 young fat turkey or chicken, weighing 6 to 7 pounds
1 pound chipolatas or other small sausages
10 thick slices bacon
12 pearl onions, peeled (see Glossary, page 263)
1 tablespoon black peppercorns
1 *bouquet garni* (see Glossary, page 259)
3 cups cold water

Preheat the oven to 425 degrees.

Stuff the chicken with chipolatas and truss it—tie it up. Lay 5 slices of bacon on the bottom of a shallow casserole, place the tied chicken on its side on the bacon, and place another 5 slices of bacon over it. Place the onions, peppercorns, and *bouquet garni* around the chicken and pour over enough water to reach 1 inch up the casserole.

Roast the chicken for 2 hours, cooking it first on one side, then the other side, then breast down, and finally breast up—½ hour in each position. Baste often.

Before serving, remove the *bouquet garni*. Be sure to degrease the juices.

Carve the bird, then if you wish, reform it carefully to create a beautiful dish. Reforming the chicken is a great notion, but not that easy to accomplish. After you have carved the breast, stack the slices back together on the breastbone—the legs and wings must be carved off and replaced.

Serves 8.

Normandy

The best time to see Normandy is in the spring, when all the trees are blossoming under a pale blue sky and the countryside resembles a huge wedding bouquet. It is a splendid, unique, and intoxicating sight. Every slope is transformed into a little corner of paradise. It is a short-lived beauty and disappears in a few weeks along with the pink and white apple blossoms.

The rest of the time Normandy is like a rich, stout woman who exposes her largesse without grace. She has too much of everything. Too much shade, too many pastures, too many streams, and alas! too much cloud. It rains nearly all the time.

This rich country is for gourmands because of its *crème fraîche*, sweet cream, and double cream. We add them to many dishes because they add an extraordinary mellowness and smooth texture.

The national soup of the peasants is the Soup *à la Graisse*— Soup Made with Fat. First I will give the recipe for the fat, and then for the soup.

Norman Fat

The proportions are quite large because it is not worth making small quantities.

For 25 pounds of beef fat, use 5 pounds pork fat.

Chop the fat up small and cook it in an iron pot over a low fire, adding:

2	bunches large leeks
12	carrots
8	large onions
5 or 6	turnips
1	parsnip
1	large bunch marjoram
1	large bunch thyme
1	large bunch parsley
1	bunch celery

Yield: 8 quarts.

Here is how to produce 1 cup of fat:

12	ounces beef fat
3	ounces pork fat
1	small leek, trimmed of root ends and tough green leaves, cut lengthwise and rinsed
2	carrots, peeled
1	onion

1 small turnip, peeled
1 small parsnip, peeled
1 half celery stalk
1 *bouquet garni* (see Glossary, page 259) made of marjoram, thyme, and parsley
¼ cup cold water
½ teaspoon *quatre épices* (see Glossary, page 263)

Dice the fat. Cut all the vegetables into 1-inch chunks and place them in a pot. Add water and bring to a simmer. Keep the pot covered over a very low fire for 5 hours.

Strain flavored fat through a sieve and squeeze through cheesecloth into a stoneware pot or jar.

Add *quatre épices* and stir often while it cools so that the spices do not end up at the bottom of the pot. Cover with a piece of parchment paper.

The fat will keep for 3 months in the refrigerator and half a year in the freezer.

Yield: 1 cup

Soup Made with Fat

2 quarts cold water
1½ pounds potatoes, peeled and cut in ½-inch cubes
3 leeks, tough green leaves removed, cut lengthwise and rinsed, chopped
1 small savoy cabbage, cut in 4 to 6 pieces
¼ pound green beans, stalk ends cut off, then cut in half
1 sprig parsley
2 tablespoons Norman Fat (see previous page)
Salt

Bring the water to a boil in a pot. Add the potatoes and leeks.

Cook for 10 minutes, then add the cabbage, the beans, and the parsley. Add the Norman Fat and bring to a rapid boil.

Don't cook the soup too long: 20 minutes in all. The vegetables must remain whole and not overcook. You do not want the soup to become a porridge. Season with salt.

You can thicken the soup with bread if you want, but it should be thick enough without it.

The best accompaniment to Soup Made with Fat is a cool glass of harsh cider served from a frosted carafe.

Serves 8.

Onion and Potato Soup

1½   pounds onions, chopped
1½   pounds potatoes, peeled and cubed
6   cups cold water
2   tablespoons potato flour or cornstarch mixed with ¼ cup water
2   tablespoons unsalted butter
½   cup heavy cream
    Salt and freshly ground black pepper

In a pot, bring the potatoes, onions, and water to a boil. Cook over moderate heat until tender—10 to 15 minutes.

Rub the soup through the medium mesh of a food mill or strainer.

Put the soup back on the fire, and add the potato flour or cornstarch and water. Stir until the soup thickens.

Just before serving add the butter, cream, and salt and pepper.

Serves 8.

Norman Sole

1   1½-pound beautiful thick sole [fluke, flounder, sole,
     lemon sole, or gray sole] — have the fishmonger
     remove the dark skin
2   tablespoons unsalted butter
     Salt and freshly ground black pepper
     Pinch of nutmeg
     Dry white wine
24 mussels (1 to 1½ pounds), cleaned (see Glossary, page
     262) or 24 shucked oysters
¼   pound peeled, cooked shrimp
2   tablespoons *beurre manie* (see Glossary, page 259)
½   cup heavy cream

Preheat the oven to 400 degrees.

Place the sole in a long oven dish with small pieces of butter
dotted down its length. Sprinkle with salt and pepper and nutmeg. Cover the sole with white wine and bake for 20 minutes.
Remember to baste it as it cooks.

Steam the mussels separately (see page 128).

When the sole is cooked, remove it from the oven and pour the
juices into a little saucepan. Add some strained mussel juice.
Keep the sole in a warm place or covered with aluminum foil as
you make the sauce.

Whisk a 2-tablespoon piece of *beurre manie* into the sauce and,
just before serving, the heavy cream.

Arrange the mussels and shrimp around your sole and pour the
sauce over. Serve hot. This dish will be even more delicious if
you substitute oysters for the mussels.

Serves 4.

Boeuf à la Mode de Caen — *Braised Beef*

3 to 4   pounds beef top or bottom round, boneless chuck,
      or eye of beef, cut in a rectangle
  1   calf's foot
  1   5-inch square piece of pork rind
  4   beef bones
  2   tablespoons olive oil
  3   tablespoons cognac
  1   bottle dry white wine [3 cups]
  1   cup cold water
 10   medium-size carrots, peeled, cut in 1-inch slices
  1   *bouquet garni* (see Glossary, page 259)
  2   tablespoons salt
      Freshly ground black pepper

To eat the beef cold
  2   cups greaseless beef or veal stock
 [1   packet powdered] gelatin

Brown the beef, calf's foot, rind, and bones with olive oil in a cast iron pot or casserole over moderate heat.

Sprinkle with cognac and flame. Add a mixture of white wine and water, so that the piece of beef is covered but not drowned. Add the carrots and the *bouquet garni* and salt and pepper.

Cover the pot with parchment paper and a lid to seal it hermetically. Let it simmer for 3 hours, turning the meat every hour.

Degrease just before serving.

If you wish to eat the beef cold, cut it in slices and put the slices in a terrine or mold, 5 inches deep, 10 inches long. Take the stock and melt the gelatin in it. Pour this over the beef and chill overnight. It will be magnificent the next day.

Serves 8.

Duck Rouennais

1   4- to 5-pound live [or dead] duck [and its liver]
     (see Note below on how to kill it)
2   shallots, minced
2   tablespoons unsalted butter
     Salt and freshly ground black pepper
2   cups red wine

[If you are at all faint of heart, skip this paragraph.]

Note: Strangle a young duck by breaking its neck or thrusting a long needle through its head where there is a little hole. If you use a needle the beast will die faster and suffer less. Pluck the feathers while the animal is still warm. Cut off the neck and wing tips. Push its feet onto its back and remove the innards; put the liver aside. Collect as much blood as you can, congealed or not.

Brown the shallots in butter. Chop the liver very finely and mix this and the blood with the shallots. Add salt and pepper.

Slip this stuffing inside the duck, sew up the opening, and arrange it on a rotisserie spit in your oven or roast the duck on a rack, in an oven pan, in a 475-degree oven for 1¼ hours, turning it often, much as a spit will do.

Serve the duck hot, *without the fat collected in the dripping pan.* If the duck is young (you can tell by its beak; it bends under pressure) and of good quality, the blood (and juices) inside the duck will be sufficient to fill the platter as you carve it.

Any bird can be safely roasted in this manner.

The sauce for the duck in other known recipes for *Canard Rouennais* is prepared by carving off the flesh and then crushing the bones in a heavy press to extract the blood and juices.

[If you do not have the blood, make a sauce by pouring away all the fat from the roasting pan, adding the red wine, and bringing to a boil. Add salt and pepper and scrape the pan well. Cook for 15 minutes and strain the sauce into a sauceboat.]

Tripe à la Mode de Caen

 3   pounds tripe, cut into 2-inch pieces
 1   calf's foot, halved by the butcher
10   carrots, peeled and sliced
 3   medium-size onions, halved and stuck with cloves
 1   bouquet of fresh thyme
 1   bay leaf
     Salt
12   black peppercorns
 2   fat leeks, use only the green leaves, rinsed
 3   cups cold water
     Caramel (see page 249)

Preheat the oven to 300 degrees.

Place a layer of sliced carrots, half the onions, the bouquet of thyme, and the bay leaf, salt, and peppercorns in a heavy casserole. Cover with a layer of tripe and one half piece of calf's foot.

Continue to fill the pot with another layer of carrots, onions, and tripe, ending with carrots on which you place a bouquet of the green leek leaves.

When the pot is full, add water to just cover. Cover with parchment paper and a lid to seal it hermetically.

Simmer for 3 to 4 hours on top of the stove, or bring to a simmer on the top of the stove and cover and bake for 4 hours.

Take off the lid, remove the leeks, color the sauce with a little [2 tablespoons] caramel, and reduce for ½ hour.

The sauce must be unctuous and golden. Serve very hot.

Serves 6 to 8.

Fried Steak

4 tablespoons unsalted butter
2 6- to 10-ounce beef steaks, sliced thin, sprinkled with salt and freshly ground black pepper
2 small onions, sliced in rings
⅔ cup beef stock mixed with 1 tablespoon potato flour or cornstarch
4 tablespoons vinegar

Melt the butter in a frying pan over moderate heat. Add the onion rings and cook until tender. Push the onions to the side and add the seasoned slices of beef.

Cook the steaks for 3 minutes on each side over a high fire, without letting the onions burn.

Add the stock mixed with potato flour and vinegar; cook for 2 minutes and serve.

Serves 2.

Matelote *Sole*

1 1-pound beautiful sole [fluke, flounder, sole, lemon sole, or gray sole] —have the fishmonger remove the dark skin
½ cup cold water

½   cup dry cider
   Salt and freshly ground black pepper
1   small bouquet parsley
2   pieces of bread, sliced ½ inch thick
1   tablespoon *beurre manie* (see Glossary, page 259)
2   tablespoons very fine bread crumbs

Preheat the oven to 425 degrees.

Lay the sole skinned-side up in an ovenproof serving dish.

Add the water and dry cider. Sprinkle with salt and pepper. Add the bouquet parsley, and place 2 pieces of sliced bread (as thick as your thumb) at each end of the dish.

Cook in the oven for 15 to 20 minutes.

Just before serving, discard the parsley. Pour the sauce carefully into a saucepan and bind it by whisking in the *beurre manie.*

When it has thickened, coat the sole with the sauce and sprinkle the top with the bread crumbs. Do not *gratinée* (put under the broiler).

Serves 2.

Sautéed Rabbit with Carrots and Onions

1   rabbit, weighing about 2¾ pounds
1   tablespoon unsalted butter
1   tablespoon bacon or pork fat
1   tablespoon sugar
4   carrots, peeled and cut in chunks
2   onions, cut in 10 wedges each
1   *bouquet garni* (see Glossary, page 259)
   Salt and freshly ground black pepper

1 cup dry white wine, chicken stock or cold water
Blood from rabbit [or 1 tablespoon cornstarch or
1 tablespoon *beurre manie* (see Glossary, page 259)]

Cut up the rabbit up as if you were making a *civet* (stew, see page 34). Melt the butter and bacon fat in a casserole over moderate heat and add the sugar.

Brown the rabbit and vegetables first, then moisten with water, wine or stock.

Add the *bouquet garni* and salt and pepper. Cook the rabbit over low heat, covered in this sauce for ¾ hour.

Before serving, place the pieces of rabbit on a hot platter. Bind the sauce left in the saucepan [with the cornstarch or *beurre manie*]. Cook gently for 3 minutes. Pour the sauce through a strainer over the rabbit.

Serves 4.

Norman Sauce for Roast Rabbit

2 medium-size onions, finely sliced
2 tablespoons unsalted butter
 Salt and freshly ground black pepper
1 cup rabbit stock, water, or red wine
 Blood from rabbit [or 1 tablespoon cornstarch mixed
 with 2 tablespoons water]

Brown the sliced onions in butter in a pan over moderate heat.

Add salt and pepper and stock, water, or red wine.

Simmer for ½ hour and then whisk in the cornstarch mixed with water. Stir until the sauce thickens.

Strain the sauce, if you wish, and serve hot.

Yield: 1 cup.

Broiled Mushrooms

1½ pounds large mushrooms [such as portobellos]
½ cup fresh bread crumbs
3 tablespoons parsley, finely chopped
    Salt and freshly ground black pepper
2 tablespoons unsalted butter, diced

Preheat the broiler.

Cut the stems off the mushrooms. Cover the undersides with a layer of bread crumbs, a little parsley, salt and pepper, and diced butter.

Broil them [or bake them in a 450-degree oven for 30 minutes]. Serve very hot.

Serves 4.

La Terrinée — *Rice Pudding*

3 quarts milk
¾ pound (2 cups) rice, well-rinsed
½ cup sugar
1 teaspoon cinnamon

Preheat the oven to 300 degrees.

Place the milk and rice in an earthenware dish. Whisk in the sugar and cinnamon.

Bake for 3 hours. Do not stir as it cooks.

After 4 hours a black skin will have formed on the top. Remove it and you will find a delicious cream underneath. Serve warm or cold with sugar and cream.

Serves 10 to 12. [To make a smaller amount of Rice Pudding, use 1 quart milk to every 4 ounces (⅔ cup) rice.]

Le Beau Ténébreux—*A Chocolate-Coated Savoy Cake*

Take a savoy cake and thinly slice off the top. Make a hollow in the cake and fill it with *crème fraîche* (see Glossary, page 260). Serve the cake coated with a thick chocolate cream. [Savoy cake is a light white sponge cake. Either buy one or make with the recipe below.]

	Unsalted butter
	Sugar
6	large eggs, separated
1	cup sugar
	Finely grated zest of 1 lemon
3½	ounces (¾ cup plus 2 tablespoons) sifted cake flour
	Pinch salt
2	tablespoons Grand Marnier or liqueur of your choice
8	ounces *crème fraîche* (see Glossary, page 260)
8	ounces semi-sweet chocolate
2	tablespoons unsalted butter

Use a cake pan, a spring-form pan, or a savarin cake pan 9 inches in diameter and at least 2½ inches high or higher (the cake will rise). Butter the bottom of the pan only and sprinkle with sugar.

Preheat the oven to 350 degrees.

Ribbon the egg yolks with the sugar—that is, whisk them together until light and pale yellow. Add the lemon zest and flour. Beat the egg whites until stiff with a pinch of salt and fold them carefully into the first mixture. Pour the batter into the cake pan.

Bake for 1 hour, checking after 55 minutes, until the cake is golden and begins to pull away from the side of the pan. Cool the cake in its pan on a rack, then unmold it. Sprinkle the top with two tablespoons of a sweet liqueur of your choice, such as

Grand Marnier—anything that goes with the lemony taste of the cake.

Slice off the top third of the cake. Slide it carefully onto a plate, a piece of cardboard, or baking sheet, and put aside. To make a hollow in the cake, cut down vertically an inch or so from the edge. Do not cut all the way down. Insert a long knife sideways into the cake halfway down, using it to release a disc of cake, which you will now remove to create a round hollow. Eat the disc of cake you have just removed!

Fill the hollow with *crème fraîche*. Replace the top third of the cake.

Melt the chocolate in a bowl over hot water, add the butter, stir well, and spread over the cake. Leave to cool. Delicious!

Serves 8 to 10.

Bourdelots—*Pastry-Covered Apples or Pears*

    1   recipe *pâté brisée* (see Glossary, page 262)
   12   ripe pears or apples, peeled or unpeeled
    2   large egg yolks diluted with 2 tablespoons cold water

Preheat the oven to 400 degrees.

Take the chilled *pâté brisée* pastry out of the refrigerator 1 hour before handling.

Roll it out with a rolling pin to a thickness of a *decime* [a tenth of a franc]—about ⅛ inch thick and cut into 12 rounds, about 6¼ inches in diameter.

Drape the dough over pear or apple, leaving the stem of the fruit sticking through the center of the dough to keep it from falling off. Cut a leaf out of the remaining dough for each and stick onto the draped dough with water.

Glaze the pastry with the egg yolks diluted with water and sprinkle heavily with sugar.

Place the *bourdelots* in a baking pan and bake for 30 minutes in a 400-degree oven.

Because pears are often too hard, poach them halfway, in advance, in some sugared water.

Serves 12.

Chausson —*Apple Turnovers*

> 1   pound [frozen] puff pastry, or make your own (see page 143)
> 2¼ cups apple puree, canned, bottled, or your own
>   Nutmeg
> 2   large egg yolks, diluted with 2 tablespoons water
>   Sugar

Preheat the oven to 400 degrees.

[Defrost the pastry and bring it close to room temperature. Roll out half the puff pastry to 13 inches by 18 inches. Cut out 6 rounds, 6¼ inches in diameter.]

Place 3 tablespoons apple puree on one half of each round of pastry. Sprinkle with nutmeg.

Brush water around the edges and fold over. Press with your fingers and then press edges with the tines of a fork.

Repeat with the rest of the pastry.

Place the turnovers on a baking sheet and brush with the egg yolk glaze; prick the tops with a fork and sprinkle quite heavily with sugar.

Bake for 20 minutes.

Serves 12.

Buckwheat Crepes

[Mix the crepe mixture 2 hours in advance of cooking the crepes.]

- 1¼ cups buckwheat flour
- 3 large eggs
- 2 tablespoons *eau-de-vie* (such as kirsch)
- 2½ cups milk
- ½ teaspoon salt
  Pinch pepper
- 2 tablespoons unsalted butter or lard

Place the flour in a bowl and make a well in the middle. Gradually whisk in the eggs, *eau-de-vie,* and milk. Beat until smooth. Add the salt and a pinch pepper and beat again. It should look like a thin porridge. [You may blend all the ingredients together in a blender if you wish.]

Melt a thin film of butter in a 12-inch frying pan over moderate heat. Swirl it around until it completely covers the pan. In lower Normandy they grease the pan with lard instead of butter.

Place a large spoonful of batter in the pan and tip it so that the batter spreads out in a very thin layer.

When the crepe has colored on one side, flip it over with a wooden palette knife.

Use butter as needed to cook the rest of the crepes.

Yield: 8 12-inch crepes.

Brittany

Brittany is a region of beauty and mystery with its blue stone roads, wayside crosses, granite rock, huge emerald-green forests, narrow fields, and meadows bordered by sloping banks, shuttered in like fortresses. The moors stretch on forever, tinted violet or yellow depending on whether they are planted with heather or gorse. The roads are sunken, and seemingly human solitary trees move as if in flight or despair. Farms spaced far apart, indifferent and silent villages, a forever changing sky, and wild seas make Brittany, of all regions, a place of deep dreams and nostalgia.

The inhabitants of this region are not like other Frenchmen in the slightest. There is something about them that is grave and deep, something that will probably never be understood, but that manifests itself in their silent manner, their long glances, and in their passionate love—I might even say in their heart-rending love—for their region. Without a doubt this country is self-sufficient and *cannot* be a country of gourmands.

Material life is not the most important thing for a Breton. Without daring to say that they feed exclusively on dreams and legends, I can say that they don't attach much importance to their food or well-being, and seem to have no desire to better themselves. This material detachment creates noble beings. Bretons are not "woolen socks" [money savers] like the Tourangeau, for example. They appear to be more easily generous, hospitable, and carefree—above all, conscientious. I don't know of another region where they give you your change with such exactness and solemnity.

But let us get back to cooking. The main characteristic of Breton cooking is, above all, the excellent quality of the materials, which must be gathered on the spot. For example, the clear pure spring water of Brittany, which flows over granite or lies still at the bottom of an icy well, naturally creates a better soup than river water that carries along with it a thousand impurities, or the hard chalky water from certain regions in which vegetables never seem to cook completely.

The rich milk from their young cows makes particularly exquisite curds. The little lambs are also exquisite (especially near the coast) where they graze on salty grasses and breathe the fresh ocean air, and whose delicate meat cannot be compared to that of any other lamb. The salted butter that is made so well by the Bretons is also widely used. Whether it is shaped in large round pats on a plate, or in stoneware pots, you can't help but dig into it incessantly. It adds a taste of hazelnut to dishes.

Finally, the best ocean fish are from Brittany, because they are of premium freshness. The taste of the sea cannot be preserved when they are shipped. These varied, numerous, sumptuous fish are just not the same even when you eat them in a port near the sea where they were caught, or when you buy them at dawn from the market towns in the center of France.

Take whiting, for instance. The simple whiting makes a sublime dish when it jumps from the bottom of a fishing boat straight into a frying pan of sizzling butter. It turns even more brilliant and iridescent, mother of pearl reflects in its scales, and its flesh is fine textured and white, as if the sea glows within — it would seem that you drink it rather than eat it. But a voyage of a few hours is enough to kill the whiting. It becomes dull, gray, pale, dry, and the flesh softens. It is difficult to revive — even a squeeze of lemon juice doesn't help.

The fish that are caught on the Breton coast besides the whiting include mackerel, bass, mullet, conger eel, tuna, *pironneau*, sole, plaice, and sardines.

The Breton Sardine

Sardine fishing is not the only resource of the coastal inhabitants, but it is still the basis of their nourishment. These beautiful sardines, which everyone has eaten from the can, are even better when fresh.

Choose 2 or 3 sardines for each serving.

Sprinkle the sardines with salt and let them sit for 1 hour after they are caught. Remove most of the salt with a clean cloth; then grill them over burning hot coals until they are crisp. Eat them just as they are with butter.

You can also fry them in salted butter in a pan over a high fire.

Serve them on a hot platter when they have turned golden brown.

Fish (Conger Eel) Soup

1   recipe for Cabbage Soup (see page 19)
2   pounds conger eel straight from the deep
    (preferably a black eel from the rocks)
    [or monkfish tail, cut into thick slices]
1   recipe for White Sauce (see page 55)

In a large pot, such as a *marmite* (see Glossary, page 262), make
Cabbage Soup.

A half hour before serving, when the soup is at a boil, add the
eel or monkfish. It will give an excellent taste to the soup.

Remove the soup from the heat. Place the eel or monkfish on a
platter and serve with the White Sauce. Eat the soup separately.

Serves 8.

Grilled or Broiled Tuna

2   10-ounce tuna steaks, 1 inch thick
2   tablespoons unsalted butter, melted
2   tablespoons parsley, finely chopped

Place the tuna over a grill of burning embers, or under a preheated broiler. Grill or broil 3 minutes on each side, basting
often with plenty of butter and parsley.

Serve this excellent fish on a hot platter.

Serves 2.

Breton Sole

1½ pounds Dover sole [gray sole, fluke, or flounder],
     skinned — have the fishmonger do this
  3 tablespoons salted butter
     Freshly ground black pepper
     Lemon juice

Slice down the length of the back with a thin knife. Fill the incision with 1 tablespoon bits of salted butter.

Cook the sole in a large frying pan in which the rest of the salted butter is already singing. The sole must be bathed in the butter. Turn it once, pepper it, and, if you want to, sprinkle with lemon juice.

Sheer perfection.

Serves 2.

Lobster and Spiny Lobster

Lobsters are found in great profusion in Brittany. For example, in a little farming town like Gúerande, which may just as well have been asleep for three centuries, not a single prefectorial arrest has been made to change the habits of the inhabitants, who blithely continue to throw the contents of their rubbish bins in the streets. You can calculate the enormous number of lobsters that have been consumed by the number of lobster shells that literally pave the streets. Even the cats show no more interest in them. Were you to offer a lobster to a poor man, he would certainly shrug his shoulders and refuse it.

However, Breton lobsters and spiny lobsters are of the best quality. Eat them cold with mayonnaise to which is added chopped parsley, and don't forget to add the soft yellow substance that you find in the head of the lobster.

1   1½- or 2-pound lobster
½   cup mayonnaise
1   tablespoon parsley, finely chopped

Steam or boil the 1½-pound lobster for 15 minutes, 25 minutes for the 2-pound lobster.

Serves 1 or 2.

[It is not advisable to add the "yellow" part of the lobster's body to the mayonnaise. Pampille is referring to the tomalley—usually greenish in color, it is the lobster's liver and nowadays may be contaminated. If the lobster is female you may add the red roe to the mayonnaise.]

Shrimp

Gray shrimp are not much appreciated in Brittany. People prefer the pink shrimp or prawns, also called *le brin.*

Cook shrimp in boiling sea (salted) water for 2 minutes and serve them with butter.

Mussels, Cockles, Clams, *and* Petoncles

Mussels are excellent in Brittany. They can't be accused of giving typhoid to anyone. Prepare cockles, clams, and *petoncles* in the same way as mussels—cooking them in a saucepan by themselves. *Petoncles* are delicious crustaceans that one can find on the Finistère coast. They are a smaller version of sea scallops and have a finer taste.

2   pounds mussels, cleaned (see Glossary, page 262)
½   cup dry white wine
2   tablespoons unsalted butter

Place the mussels and wine in a large pot with a lid on moderate fire. They will open in about 5 minutes and cook in their own juice. When they are cooked, discard the empty shell of each mussel and arrange them on a round platter. Discard any mussels that don't open.

Eat them with fresh butter [or melt butter in the juices].

Serves 4

Scallops

Prepare these excellent crustaceans in the following manner:

Wash and scrape the shells well.

Open them by heating them slightly on the stove top. Remove the fringe around the central muscle. Put the roe, known as the coral—it resembles a little pink-orange tongue—aside. [Fresh scallops in the shell with their roe can still be found in European fish stores. The scallop and its roe are sometimes found on the East Coast of the United States and others are imported from Europe.]

    1 pound sea scallops with roe, if available
       [cut in ¾-inch cubes]
    1 cup fresh bread crumbs
    2 tablespoons parsley, chopped
    1 small onion, finely chopped
    3 tablespoons unsalted butter
       Salt and freshly ground black pepper
       Pinch cayenne pepper
    4 scallop shells or small ovenproof plates or bowls

Preheat the oven to 400 degrees.

Brown the bread crumbs, parsley, and onion in the butter. Season with salt, pepper, and cayenne pepper. Divide the scallops and their roe into the scallop shells, plates, or bowls and top with the flavored bread crumbs.

Bake for 15 minutes.

Serves 4.

Breton Andouille *Sausages*

If fish have taken first place among the finest products of Brittany, then the second place goes to pigs. Their hides are usually black. These small pigs go about in groups in the fields. You see them running about searching for food, drinking from ponds, and rolling around in the mud and manure, to justify their reputation.

Their flesh is good to eat, although it has a kind of wild odor that not everyone likes. The Bretons make excellent *andouille* sausages with the pigs' stomach linings. They are quite different from the *andouille* sausages from the center of France, because the innards are inserted one into another to form a compact homogenous mass.

When the *andouilles* have been prepared, they are hung from Breton chimneys (short flues and very large fireplaces), where they smoke for several months. Let me add that the Bretons burn only wood or dry gorse in this chimney. The *andouilles* are covered with saltpeter, blacken, and become hard as a walking stick.

When the Bretons want to eat them, they take them down and soak them in cold water for 24 hours, changing the water several times to get rid of the saltpeter. Then they wrap them with hay and boil them for several hours in a *marmite* (see Glossary, page 262). Eat *andouilles* hot, preferably with a potato puree, or sauté slices of the *andouilles* with butter in a frying pan.

Poultry Stuffing for Fat Birds

1   4- to 6-pound roasting chicken
1¾ pounds peeled roasted chestnuts, fresh or canned
4   prunes, seeded and chopped
¼   cup raisins
¾   pound sausage meat, sautéed with 2 tablespoons
    unsalted butter
4   chicken livers, chopped
1   large egg, beaten
    Salt and freshly ground black pepper

Preheat the oven to 425 degrees.

Make a stuffing by mixing the chestnuts, prunes, raisins, sausage meat, chicken livers, and salt and pepper.

Stuff a bird, tie it up—truss it—and roast it for 1½ to 2 hours. This stuffing is very filling.

Serves 6.

Breton Leg of Lamb

Pre-sale leg of lamb with white beans is the name given to a leg of lamb Breton style. This lamb is very small, but as I mentioned, it has a particularly delicate flesh.

2   cloves garlic, slivered lengthwise
1   leg of lamb
    Unsalted butter
    Salt and freshly ground black pepper
1   pound large dried white beans
2   onions, quartered
1   *bouquet garni* (see Glossary, page 259)

4   whole cloves garlic
2   onions, finely chopped
2   shallots, minced
2   large tomatoes, roughly chopped—in winter replace
    them with bottled or canned tomatoes

Soak the white beans (called *Soissons beans*) in a bowl of plenty
of cold water overnight.

Place 2 halved onions, *bouquet garni*, garlic, salt and pepper,
and drained beans in a pot. Add water to cover by 3 inches and
bring slowly to a boil. Simmer for 1 hour, until the beans are
tender, and drain them in a colander.

Preheat the oven to 400 degrees.

Stick small slivers of garlic in the leg, rub it with butter, sprinkle it with pepper, and roast it for 1½ hours.

[If you like your lamb pink in the middle, take it out of the
oven when an instant-read thermometer inserted in the center
of the leg reads 120 degrees. Do not turn the oven off.]

Place 3 tablespoons butter in a saucepan over moderate to low
heat and add the chopped onions, shallots, and tomatoes. Let
them cook slowly, stirring occasionally until it becomes a light
puree.

Add the juices from the roast lamb to the puree just before
serving. Add the beans to this concentrated sauce. Blend together, being careful not to crush the beans.

When the beans have absorbed the puree somewhat, pour
them into an oven dish. Place the leg of lamb on top of the
beans and reheat in the oven for another 10 minutes. [Let stand
15 minutes before carving.]

Serves 8.

Buckwheat Crepes

To make these buckwheat crepes successfully, you have to have a Breton chimney, a Breton fire, a Breton *galetière* (the *galetière* is a flat edgeless griddle with a small handle), a Breton wooden spatula, a Breton scraper, Breton wheat, a Breton cook, and a Breton soul. When all these conditions have been met, one can start to make the crepes.

Use batter recipe for Buckwheat Crepes on page 122.

Put the *galetière* (pan without edges) or 12-inch frying pan on a gorse fire or stove top over moderate heat. Place a knob of butter as big as a walnut (1½ tablespoons) on it and let it melt and start to sizzle. Pour a soup ladle of batter onto the *galetière*.

The crepe must be made in three movements:

1. Use a scraper to spread the batter onto the *galetière*.
2. With a wooden spatula, turn the crepes as they brown.
3. As they cook, take them off the heat quickly and place them on a wooden tray. Pile them one on top of the other.

These crepes are excellent served hot with sugar or milk curds. They are even better with an egg broken inside and folded in quarters like a handkerchief. Reheat them with a little butter on the *galetière*.

You must drink a pitcher of cider with these Breton crepes.

Yield: 8 12-inch crepes

Le Lait Ribaud — *Laughing Milk*

Ah! You have to be a Breton to like this milk. It is made from
pale white cooked milk curds. They have a rubbery consistency
and a smoky aftertaste. I don't advise strangers to try them.

More Desserts

To finish the desserts, let me mention the flan, and the *craque-
lins* from Lanvillon (North Coast Brittany). These are small
thick brown cakes, shaped like the hollow of your hand, with
little holes underneath. Dipped into milk, fried in butter, and
sprinkled with sugar, they are a true nicety.

Burgundy, Lyonnaise Region

[Nearly all the recipes in this section are from a recipe book by M. Lucien Tendret, a lawyer at Belley, *La Table au Pays de Brillat-Savarin,* Bailly Fils, publishers at Belley, 1892.]

Braised Leg of Lamb with Onions

A leg of lamb, young chickens, or ducklings cooked in this manner make a delicious meal. The taste of the onions is not too strong, but sweet and sugary, like a *soubise*. [*Soubise* is a luscious preparation made from onions cooked with rice for a long time, until a puree is formed.] The author of this recipe adds: "When the guests are tempted to come back for more, they find that the braise has been reduced to leftovers, attesting both to the excellence of the dish, and its largesse."

    1   leg of lamb
    3   small onions, quartered
   3¾   cups beef stock
        Salt and freshly ground black pepper
    ½   cup water
    ½   cup tomato sauce
    2   10-ounce boxes pearl onions, peeled
        (see Glossary, page 263)
    2   tablespoons unsalted butter
    1   tablespoon sugar
    ½   cup *jus* (see page 47)
    1   tablespoon cornstarch dissolved in 1 tablespoon cold
        beef stock

Place the leg of lamb in a braising pan—a large heavy casserole with a lid about 15 inches in diameter to fit the leg of lamb. Add the onions and ¾ cup beef stock, salt and pepper. Simmer for 1 hour and 10 minutes.

Remove the onions and any remaining stock—reserve. Raise the fire to brown the meat. Turn the leg so it can brown all over.

Add the water, 2 cups stock, and the tomato sauce. Let simmer.

In the meantime, sauté the onions in butter. Sprinkle with sugar, add 1 cup stock and the *jus*, and let reduce for 10 minutes. Pour the onions and their juices back into the braising pan with the leg of lamb.

It must cook for 1 to 1½ hours from the moment it is placed on the fire. Check for doneness after 1 hour. [An instant-read thermometer should read 120 degrees for pink in the middle, or 140 degrees for cooked all the way through.]

Before serving, put the lamb on a warm platter and surround it with the onions. Thicken the sauce by adding the cornstarch dissolved in water.

Serves 8.

Stuffed Calf's Ears

[If you can find calf's ears, fine and good—I have adapted this recipe for use with veal scallops, held together with toothpicks to look very similar to calf's ears.]

Blanch the calf's ears and wash them carefully. Rub them with lemon juice and wrap them in little bags made with cheesecloth.

Place the ears in a saucepan containing equal quantities of white wine and beef stock. Add an onion, a carrot, chervil, parsley, thyme, and salt and pepper.

Bring to a boil and cook for 3 hours, making sure to add more white wine and stock as it evaporates, so that the ears are always covered with liquid. When they are cooked, drain them.

[8 veal scallops, about 1 pound]

Stuffing
- 1 pound sweetbreads or calf brains, cooked
- 1 pound chicken breasts, cooked
- 6 tablespoons unsalted butter
- 2 tablespoons all-purpose flour
- 1 cup *jus* (see page 47)
- ¼ cup *crème fraîche* (see Glossary, page 260)
- 1 black truffle, finely chopped [1 tablespoon black truffle puree (Salsa Tartufata by Urbani, see Sources, page 265), 1 teaspoon white truffle oil, or 12 ounces very finely chopped mushrooms, sautéed with butter until they lose their moisture and become very dark]

    Salt and freshly ground black pepper
1 large egg yolk mixed with ¼ cup heavy cream
3 large egg whites
1½ cups fresh bread crumbs
2 tablespoons olive oil

Cut cooked sweetbreads and chicken breasts into little cubes. Fry the cubes over moderate heat in 4 tablespoons butter. When they have browned, sprinkle with flour and stir in the *jus*.

When the mixture is thick and smooth, add the *crème fraîche*, minced black truffles, black truffle puree, white truffle oil or mushrooms and remove from the fire.

After 2 minutes, stir in the egg yolk and cream mixture. Let cool.

Pound the veal scallops thin and wrap them one by one around the filling, making closed triangular shapes. Fix with toothpicks.

Beat the egg whites until stiff. Dip the scallops into the egg whites and then into the bread crumbs.

Fry them gently in 2 tablespoons butter and 2 tablespoons olive oil until golden.

Preheat the oven to 400 degrees.

To serve, reheat the "ears" in the oven for 15 minutes. Remove the toothpicks before serving.

Serve with mayonnaise or a béarnaise sauce (pages 51 and 56).

Yield: 8 "ears"— serves 4 to 8.

Steamed Truffled Bresse Hen

1 7-pound chicken—a pretty hen with fine white
   fat skin and black or gray feet
   Salt
½ pound cubed black truffles [or 1 jar black truffle puree
   (such as Salsa Tartufata by Urbani, see Sources, page
   265)]
4 chicken livers, including 1 from the chicken, chopped
   Chicken fat, taken from the opening to the cavity,
   chopped and rendered
⅓ cup cognac
   Freshly ground black pepper
½ lemon
   Cheesecloth
5 cups chicken stock
1½ cups dry white wine
   Parchment paper
3 tablespoons unsalted butter
2 tablespoons all-purpose flour
½ cup heavy cream
2 large egg yolks stirred into ½ cup heavy cream

Salt the inside of the chicken.

Wash, dry, and peel the truffles, cut them in cubes the size of a hazelnut, and mix them with chopped chicken livers. Sauté this mixture in the chicken fat over moderate heat.

Sprinkle with cognac and flame. Add salt and pepper.

Stuff the chicken with this mixture.

[Note: If not using the truffles, loosen the chicken skin from the neck end carefully with your fingers. Avoid tearing the skin. Insert 2 tablespoons black truffle puree under the chicken skin over the breast and thighs.] Sauté the chicken livers in chicken fat. Add 3 tablespoons black truffle puree and 2 tablespoons cognac; flame. Fill the cavity of the chicken with this stuffing and rub with lemon juice.

Wrap the chicken in cheesecloth and wait an hour while the aroma of the truffles perfumes its flesh.

Place an iron trivet at the bottom of a *pot-au-feu* [or use a vegetable steamer in the bottom of a 16-quart pot]. Pour in the stock and white wine. Rub the chicken with lemon juice and place it on the trivet. The liquid must not touch the chicken. Seal the pot hermetically with parchment paper and the lid. Simmer over low heat for 1½ hours.

Make a *roux* (see Glossary, page 263) using 3 tablespoons butter and 2 tablespoons flour, moistening it with the heavy cream.

Remove the chicken from the *pot-au-feu*, place on a platter, and remove the cheesecloth.

Finish the sauce by adding 1½ cups liquid from the pot, and salt and pepper to the *roux*. Heat and then thicken the sauce further by adding the egg yolks and cream mixture. Serve with the chicken.

Fat poultry is best steamed rather than boiled in a stock.

[Note: If you want to crisp the skin, roast the chicken in a 450-degree oven for 20 minutes.]

Serves 6.

Chicken Fricassee — with Onions, Thyme, and Cream

You can enrich this delicious dish with crawfish, fresh morels, or artichoke bottoms. [See Sources, page 265 for crawfish sources.]

2 3- to 4-pound chickens, cut *selon les règles* [according
   to the custom—each breast in half and each thigh
   and drumstick separated, plus the back, for a total of
   nine pieces, see Glossary, page 260]
4 tablespoons unsalted butter
2 medium-size onions, coarsely chopped
5 sprigs fresh thyme
   Salt
1½ tablespoons all-purpose flour
½ cup cold water
2½ cups heavy cream
½ cup dry white wine
   Pinch freshly ground black pepper
2 large egg yolks, mixed with ¼ cup heavy cream

Optional garnish:
   Crawfish tails, peeled and sautéed in butter or fresh
   morels or artichoke bottoms

Sauté the chicken pieces and onions in the butter in a heavy
casserole over a moderate fire. Add thyme and salt, and when
the chicken pieces are browned, sprinkle in the flour.

Add the water and scrape the bottom and sides of the pan to
get all the browned bits—called *les sucs.*

Pour ½ cup heavy cream and the dry white wine into the fricassee and simmer for 5 minutes.

Add the rest of the cream little by little, and cook until the
sauce thickens and coats the back of a spoon.

Simmer for another 25 to 35 minutes, until the chicken is tender. Taste the sauce and add freshly ground pepper. Whisk in
the egg yolks and cream mixture. Heat over a very low fire until
the sauce has thickened. Do not let boil.

Serves 8.

Celestine's Chicken

The celebrated *Café du Cercle* in Lyon has served this dish for 50 years. Rousselot, the chef, was a brilliant sauce maker. Here is his recipe for Celestine's Chicken.

>   1   3- to 4-pound chicken, cut *selon les règles* [according to the custom—each breast in half and each thigh and drumstick separated, plus the back, for a total of nine pieces, see Glossary, page 260]
>   4   tablespoons unsalted butter
>   4   ounces button mushrooms, sliced
>   1   medium-size ripe tomato, seeded and cut in small cubes
>   ¾   cup dry white wine
>   ½   cup *jus* (see page 47)
> 1 to 2   tablespoons cognac
>   Salt and pepper
>   Pinch cayenne pepper
>   1   tablespoon parsley, finely chopped
>   1   garlic clove, minced

Heat the butter in a pan until it turns golden. Add the chicken pieces and brown them over a moderate fire.

Add the sliced mushrooms and the cubed tomato. Sauté for 5 minutes, then add the white wine, the *jus*, cognac, salt and pepper, and a touch of cayenne. Cook for another 15 minutes.

Place the chicken on a hot platter. Degrease the sauce and reduce somewhat, sprinkle with chopped parsley and minced garlic. Cook for another 2 minutes.

Pour the sauce over the chicken and serve.

Serves 4.

The Meat Pies of Bugey

These delicious little meat pies are eaten only on Christmas Eve. Bakers and pastry cooks take them scorching hot out of their ovens after midnight mass, so they can warm the stomachs of the faithful.

1 recipe puff pastry [see below]
5 ounces tripe, chopped quite fine, cooked in a *court-bouillon* (see Glossary, page 260) for 3 hours [or 5 ounces cooked sausage meat]
9 ounces cooked turkey meat, cubed
1 onion, chopped and sautéed in 1 tablespoon butter until translucent
Salt and freshly ground black pepper
½ cup turkey *jus*, (see page 47)
3 tablespoons raisins
1 large egg yolk mixed with 1 tablespoon water

Puff Pastry
Start making at least 3 hours or the day before needed

Primary dough
¾ pound (2¼ cups) all-purpose flour
¼ pound (¾ cup) cake flour
1 tablespoon salt
4 ounces (1 stick) unsalted butter, cut in thin slices
¾ cup cold water

Butter mixture
1¼ pounds unsalted butter, softened
¼ pound (¾ cup) cake flour

Make the *primary dough* first. [Process the flours and salt for 2 seconds in a food processor. Add sliced butter and process for 10 seconds until crumbly. Add the cold water and process until it begins to form a whole. Take the dough out, and knead into a 12-inch square about 1 inch thick. Cover with plastic wrap and refrigerate.

To make the dough by hand: Place the flour on a board in the shape of a crown. Put the salt and water in the middle. Stir so that the flour gradually mixes together with the liquid and a homogenous mass is formed. Knead and add the butter (in this case coarsely grated) for a few minutes, then knead as above.

To make the *butter mixture,* knead the butter in a bowl, adding the cake flour. Shape this butter into a shape about 9 inches square, cover with plastic wrap, and refrigerate.

When both the dough and the butter mixture are at more or less the same pliability (20 to 30 minutes), lay the dough onto a floured surface and roll the 4 corners out so they are thinner than the rest of the dough. Place the butter in the center and fold over the corners of the dough so that the butter is completely covered. Roll out to a length of 15 inches and a width of about 7 inches, the length of the rectangle stretching away from you. Note: If you ever see signs that the butter may break through, or the dough becomes very elastic, abandon the rolling pin and throw the dough back into the refrigerator, covered as before.

Fold the rectangle of dough into thirds. Turn the dough so the side edges face you. Roll the dough out again into a long rectangle and fold into thirds again. Now make two impressions in the dough with your finger. You have made two "turns" — rolled and folded two times. Make four to five more "turns," always throwing the dough back in the refrigerator to rest for an hour or so if it shows signs of becoming too soft or too elastic to roll.

Refrigerate covered for a couple hours before using, or even better, overnight.]

For the stuffing
Mix the cooked tripe or sausage meat with the onion sautéed in butter, the turkey meat, salt and pepper, turkey *jus,* and the raisins to make a pie filling.

Preheat the oven to 400 degrees.

Finally, roll the dough out to a thickness of ¼ inch and cut into 24 rectangles (4 inches by 3 inches).

Place 2 tablespoons of filling on 12 of the rectangles. Top with remaining rectangles and brush the edges with water. Seal the edges, pressing them together with your fingers.

Glaze the pies with egg yolks and water.

Place them on baking sheets.

Bake for 25 minutes, in batches. Serve them hot.

Yield: 12 *meat pies.*

Crawfish Nantua Style

5 dozen live crawfish [see Sources, page 265, for crawfish sources]
  Boiling water
6 ounces unsalted butter
1 tablespoon all-purpose flour
1 cup *crème fraîche* (see Glossary, page 260)

Throw the crawfish into boiling water. Cook for 5 minutes. Drain them.

Shell the crawfish tails.

Crush the shells in the food processor or chop small.

Simmer the shells very gently in butter for 5 minutes. The butter should be pink.

Drain the butter into a pan. Add the flour and stir. Add 1 cup *crème fraîche.* Stir and cook for another 3 to 4 minutes. Add salt and pepper and stir the crawfish tails into the sauce.

Serve in small scallop shells.

[You can use 2½ cups cooked shelled crawfish tails (see Sources, page 265) and make a sauce as above. It won't taste as good because the butter has not been flavored with the shells.]

Serves 5.

The Fondue of Belley

According to Brillat-Savarin, in his *Physiologie du Goût,* "The fondue is originally Swiss. It is nothing but scrambled eggs with cheese, the amount of which depends on time and experience."

To succeed with this dish, so appreciated by Brillat-Savarin, you must have eggs that were laid the morning of the day you want to use them. Also fresh butter, excellent Gruyère, and some round odiferous black truffles.

> 3 truffles [or 3 tablespoons black truffle puree
>   (Salsa Tartufata by Urbani, see Sources, page 265)
>   or 1 teaspoon white truffle oil]
> 6 tablespoons unsalted butter
>   Salt and freshly ground black pepper
> 6 large eggs, separated

4   ounces Gruyère cheese, finely grated
6   tablespoons turkey or meat *jus* (see page 47)
    Freshly ground black pepper

Wash the truffles and peel them. Dice them finely.

Sauté them very gently in 2 tablespoons butter for 5 minutes. Sprinkle with salt and pepper and put aside to cool.

Beat the egg whites. When they are stiff, gradually add the yolks, then 2 tablespoons butter, cut in thin slices, the grated Gruyère, and finally the truffles.

Pour ½ cup turkey or meat *jus* in a large frying pan and place on moderate heat. When it is boiling, pour in the egg mixture, whisking it lightly.

When the mixture starts to thicken, take the pan off the fire and continue to whisk until you obtain a smooth cream.

Add 2 tablespoons *jus*, and 2 tablespoons butter, cut in thin slices.

Put the fondue on the fire again to finish the cooking.

The fondue must remain creamy. Pepper it and serve without delay.

Serves 2.

The Black Morels of Valromey

Morel mushrooms, which make a brief appearance in spring-time, when properly prepared are some of the best mushrooms that you can eat. Black morels are better than white morels, as they are smaller and more aromatic.

1   pound morels
3   tablespoons unsalted butter
2   tablespoons all-purpose flour
3   tablespoons *jus* (see page 47) or strong beef stock
2   cups heavy cream
    Salt and freshly ground black pepper
2   large egg yolks diluted with ¼ cup heavy cream

Before cooking the morels, you must cut off the end of the stalks and slice them in half lengthwise. Wash them in cold water, because they often contain sand, which grates against your teeth. Get rid of the grit by cleaning them in several changes of water, then drain them.

Place the morels in a pan with the butter and sauté them over moderate heat until they become tender and lose their moisture.

Lower the heat and sprinkle the morels with the flour. Stir and add the *jus* or stock, and then gradually pour in 2 cups heavy cream. Add salt and pepper. Simmer for 15 minutes.

Whisk in the egg yolks and cream mixture, and heat without boiling, until the sauce thickens.

Serves 6 to 8.

Franche-Comté

Panade

This is an essential dish in Comtois cuisine, probably made for the not-so-well-off. Make it in a shallow earthenware casserole.

It is hard to think of anyone who would enjoy the *panade*; it is nothing but a gruel of bread and water. However, it is used in *Oulade* and *Garbure* (see pages 204 and 227). Another version of *panade* is used in the *Quenelles* recipe, but that one is made of bread crumbs and milk.

    5 thick crustless slices bread, dried out
    5 cups boiling water
    2 tablespoons unsalted butter

Line the casserole with the slices of bread. Cover the bread with boiling water and bring to a slow boil, so the bread does not rise up and overflow. Regulate the fire to simmer. Cook for about ¾ hour.

A quarter hour before the end of the cooking, stir the mixture with a wooden spoon to loosen up the bread. Add the butter and serve.

Serves 2.

Frog Legs Stock

This stock should be the color of straw and have such a fine taste that it can be mistaken, even by connoisseurs, for chicken stock. Use as a base for soups.

> 2 pounds frogs legs (see Sources, page 265)
> 2 leeks, halved lengthwise, rinsed and sliced
> 3 carrots, scraped and sliced
> 2 medium white turnips, peeled and cubed
> 2 parsnips, peeled and sliced
> 3 quarts water

To achieve a fine stock, place the frog legs, similar to the recipe for *Pot-au-Feu* (see page 14), in cold salted water and bring to a boil. Skim carefully.

Add what the Comtois call the *savor*—sliced leeks, carrots, turnips, and parsnips—to flavor the stock.

When it comes to a boil again, moderate the fire so that the stock simmers. You will need 1½ to 2 hours or more to obtain a perfect stock.

Do not cover the stock as this will prevent reduction.

Yield: 1 quart.

Les Gaudes — *Polenta*

This is a good dish to serve on Fridays.

- 3 cups cold water
- 1 cup coarse cornmeal or polenta
- 2 tablespoons unsalted butter
  Salt
- 8 ounces *crème fraîche* (see Glossary, page 260)

Bring the water to a boil in a saucepan. Pour in the cornmeal gradually, stirring all the time with a wooden spoon or whisk.

Turn the fire very low and continue to stir every few minutes. Add the butter and salt. Cook for 25 minutes.

Add the *crème fraîche* and then pour the mixture into an 8-inch tart, pie pan or similar pan.

Cut in slices and fry the *gaudes* in a little butter or oil until browned.

Serves 6.

Macaroni Timbale

[This macaroni pie is reminiscent of the splendid Sicilian macaroni pie described in *Il Gattopardo* by Lampedusa — a wonderful story of Sicilian aristocracy in the nineteenth century.]

- 1 recipe *pâté brisée* (see Glossary, page 262)
- 8 tablespoons unsalted butter
- 4 tablespoons all-purpose flour
- 2 cups *jus* (see page 47)
- 2 cups tomato sauce (see page 49)
  Salt and freshly ground black pepper

  1   teaspoon *quatre épices* (see Glossary, page 263)
  ½   pound Gruyère cheese, grated
  ½   pound thick sliced ham, cubed
  ½   pound sliced cooked tongue [or cooked chicken breast]
  ½   pound [button mushrooms] or morels, quartered and cooked
  ½   pound cooked sweetbreads [or calf brains, cut in pieces]
  1   pound macaroni [elbows or *penne*]
  1   large egg yolk, mixed with 1 tablespoon water

Optional garnish:
    Quenelles (see page 153) and cooked crawfish (see page 145)

In a large saucepan over low heat, make a white *roux* (see Glossary, page 263) — use 8 tablespoons butter and 4 tablespoons flour and blend it with the *jus*. Add the tomato sauce, salt and pepper, *quatre épices*, and Gruyère cheese.

Place the saucepan over a moderate fire. When the cheese has melted and the sauce has become thick enough to coat the back of a wooden spoon, add the ham, tongue or chicken, morel or button mushrooms, and sweetbreads or brains.

Cook the macaroni in boiling salted water, following the directions on the package, until tender. When it is cooked, strain. Add to the above mixture of sauce and meats. Taste for seasoning, to make sure the flavors are distinct.

Preheat the oven to 400 degrees.

Place macaroni mixture in a deep ovenproof dish or a shallow earthenware casserole. Moisten the edges of the dish with water.

Roll out the pastry *(pâte brisée)* to fit the top. Flute the edges deco-ratively. Brush the pastry with an egg yolk mixed with water and prick the top with a fork in 4 or 5 places.

Bake the pie for 30 to 40 minutes.

Serves 10.

Quenelles — *Pike Forcemeat*

Pike fish *quenelles* were invented by Bontemps, the celebrated Comptois chef. They are used as a garnish around chicken breasts, or in *vol-au-vents.* They are not like the *quenelles* made in Paris, which usually have veal or udder as a base. [!]
   [A Nantua sauce, made with crawfish, is the finest accompaniment (see page 145).] •

   ½   pound boneless, skinless pike fillet or whiting
          Panade made from 2¼ cups fresh bread crumbs,
          ⅓ cup milk, and 1 large egg yolk
   ½   pound unsalted butter, softened
   1   small *bouquet garni* (see Glossary, page 259)
          Salt and freshly ground white pepper
          [Optional sauce: Sauce Nantua (see page 145)]

Use equal proportions of pike, *panade,* and butter.

Rub the pike fillet flesh through a sieve. Add salt and pound it for 8 to 10 minutes.

Blend the pike and the *panade* together by pounding for 10 minutes.

When the pike/*panade* mixture is smooth, add to the softened butter and mix well.

Place the *quenelle* mixture on a board sprinkled with flour.

Using a knife dipped in hot water, shape and cut the mixture into small squares.

Bring a pot of water to a simmer with the *bouquet garni* and salt. Add the *quenelles*, in batches. Let them cook and swell up for a few minutes, then drain.

The *quenelles* are ready to eat.

[*Alternative Method*

Instead of all the pushing through sieves and pounding required in the old days, be thankful for the food processor!

Grind the pike fillet in the food processor.

Mix the bread crumbs, milk, and yolk to make the *panade*.

Process the fish, *panade*, and butter in the food processor with some salt and pepper.

Bring a pot of water to a simmer with the *bouquet garni* and salt. Lower the heat so that the water barely moves. Shape the *quenelles* with two dessert spoons and drop them in simmering water for 2 minutes each.

Drain on paper towels.

They can be made in advance and reheated briefly in hot water.]

Yield: about 30 quenelles.

The True Woodcock Salmis — *Stew*

It is usual to hang game such as woodcock in a cold place for a few days, in order to tenderize them and give them a stronger, or "high," taste.

[2 small cornish hens, cut in 4 pieces, livers saved
   or 4 woodcocks, de-feathered and innards saved]
3 thick slices bacon, cut in 1-inch pieces
1 medium-size onion, chopped
3 shallots, minced
1 *bouquet garni* (see Glossary, page 259)
1 clove
12 juniper berries, crushed
2 tablespoons unsalted butter
3 cloves garlic
1 tablespoon all-purpose flour
1¾ cups red wine
   Olive oil

Preheat the oven to 450 degrees.

Roast the cornish hens for 45 minutes or the woodcocks for 20 minutes.

Brown the bacon in a pan with the onions, shallots, *bouquet garni*, clove, and juniper berries in the butter over moderate heat. Brown the cornish hen pieces or woodcocks with the garlic. Add the flour and red wine and simmer for 20 minutes. Remove the pieces of hen or woodcock and put aside in a warm place.

Pound the livers with a few drops of olive oil and add to the sauce. Reduce the sauce until it coats the back of a wooden spoon. Push the sauce through a sieve over the cornish hens or woodcocks.

Serves 2.

Potée — *Bacon and Vegetable Soup*

2½   pounds slab bacon, cut in 6-inch square pieces
  8   small red bliss potatoes
  1   small savoy cabbage, cored and cut in 12 wedges
  4   carrots, peeled and thickly sliced
       Cold water
  ½   pound green beans, trimmed, each bean cut in two
  3   tablespoons unsalted butter or lard
  8   thin slices of bread

Put the slab bacon, potatoes, cabbage, and carrots in a *pot-au-feu*. Add water and bring to a boil. Cook for 20 minutes, then add the green beans and cook for 10 more minutes.

Remove the vegetables with a slotted spoon and set aside. Continue to simmer the bacon in the soup for another 1½ hours or until tender.

Melt the butter or lard in a pan and add the vegetables. Cook for 2 minutes.

Place half the vegetables on a platter with the bacon on top.

When serving the soup, reheat the rest of the vegetables in it and ladle it over thin slices of bread.

Serves 8.

Matefaim *or* Matafam — *Sweet Fritters*

  3   large eggs
       Salt
  6   tablespoons sugar
  2   cups all-purpose flour

½ cup milk
2 tablespoons *eau-de-vie* or 1 teaspoon orange-flower
water
Deep-frying vegetable oil
Confectioner's sugar

Beat the eggs, salt, sugar, and milk together.

Place the flour in a bowl. Make a well in it and add the egg and milk mixture gradually, whisking until the batter is smooth.

Whisk in the *eau-de-vie* or orange-flower water.

Heat 2 inches of frying oil in a pan to 365 degrees. Fry tablespoons of the batter for 2 to 3 minutes each, as you would make *beignets* (fritters).

Turn them, and when they are golden, lift them out.

Serve *matefaim* warm, sprinkled with confectioner's sugar.

Serves 6.

Fromagerè

To tell the truth, this is not a great dish.

1 quart milk
½ cup boiling water
4 tablespoons unsalted butter
Salt and freshly ground black pepper

Place the milk in a bowl and leave on the kitchen counter until part of it solidifies and separates from the whey (a clear liquid), about a day. Line a sieve with a double thickness of cheesecloth.

Place the sieve above a container and pour the milk solids into it. Drain for a day. Keep the "curds" and discard the whey.

Place the crumbly curd mixture into a terrine or small bowl. Keep it in a warm place (some housewives put the terrine in their beds), stirring it often during the following days until it becomes yellow and starts to smell strong.

Now put the cheese in a saucepan on a low fire. Add boiling water, butter, and salt and pepper to make a smooth batter.

Pour this mixture, the *quincoyote*, on plates or in bowls. Serve it hot or cold as you desire. You can keep it for a month.

Serves 2.

Alsace

Choucroute

3 pounds sauerkraut, rinsed in several changes of water
1 pound lean smoked bacon or pork, sliced in ½-inch-thick strips
1 pound sausages [frankfurters, boudins, or Italian sausage]
½ pound dry garlic sausage, cut in thick slices
3 tablespoons goose fat [or vegetable oil]
8 juniper berries
1 cup dry white wine
1 cup chicken stock

Preheat the oven to 350 degrees.

Place the rinsed sauerkraut and the rest of the ingredients in an earthenware or cast iron pot. Cover with a lid and bake for 1½ hours.

Serves 6.

Ham, Baked in Crust

[Choose a country ham. See Sources, page 265.]

> 1   salt-cured ham, weighing 10 to 15 pounds
> 4   quarts dry apple cider
>   Cold water
> 3   pounds store-bought bread or pizza dough

Having desalted the ham in several changes of fresh water for 1 to 3 days, boil it in cider and water for 2 hours.

Preheat the oven to 450 degrees.

Drain and pat the ham dry.

Remove most of the fat. Wrap the ham completely with dough.

Send it to the baker to be baked in his oven or bake for 1 hour in your oven.

Ham cooked by this method remains very juicy.

Serves 15.

Bakenofe—
A Casserole of Pork and Lamb, Onion, and Potato

>   Unsalted butter
> 2   large onions, sliced
> 1½ pounds potatoes, peeled and sliced

1 carrot, peeled and sliced
6 parsley sprigs
1 small bay leaf
1 pound each pork chops and lamb shoulder chops,
  cut ½ inch thick
  Salt and freshly ground black pepper
¾ cup dry white wine

Preheat the oven to 375 degrees.

Butter a heavy casserole or pot with a lid. Place a layer of sliced onions on the bottom, then a layer of sliced potatoes, sliced carrot, parsley sprigs, and bay leaf. Then add pork and lamb chops. Add salt and pepper and another layer of sliced potatoes. Pour in white wine and cover.

Take the *bakenofe* to the baker or bake for 2 hours in your own oven.

Serves 6.

Onion Tart

1 recipe *pâté brisée* (see Glossary, *pâté brisée I*, page 262)
1 bunch of young onions with their green tops or
  4 bunches scallions, finely sliced
3 tablespoons unsalted butter
  Salt
3 large eggs
½ cup *crème fraîche* (see Glossary, page 260)
4 ounces bacon, cut in 1-inch pieces, cooked until crisp

Preheat the oven to 400 degrees.

Line a 9-inch tart tin with the pastry. Press aluminum foil on top of the pastry. Bake for 20 minutes, uncovering the pastry in the last 5 minutes.

Turn the oven heat down to 350 degrees.

Sauté the onions in butter, season with salt, and place on the baked pastry.

Beat the eggs with *crème fraîche* and pour over the onions. Add the bacon.

Bake for 35 to 40 minutes.

Serves 4 to 6.

Tarte au Fromage Blanc —*White Cheese Tart*

1 recipe *pâté brisée* (see Glossary, *pâté brisée I*, page 262)
1 pound *fromage blanc* [from fancy supermarkets or specialty stores, or farmer's cheese, or low-fat cream cheese]
5 tablespoons *crème fraîche* (see Glossary, page 260)
2 large eggs, beaten
5 tablespoons all-purpose flour
   Salt and freshly ground black pepper
4 thick slices bacon, cut in 1-inch pieces, cooked until crisp
1 tablespoon unsalted butter, diced

Preheat the oven to 400 degrees.

Line a 9-inch tart tin with the pastry. Press aluminum foil on top of the pastry. Bake for 20 minutes, uncovering the pastry in the last 5 minutes. Do not turn off the oven.

Rub *fromage blanc* or farmer's cheese through a fine sieve. Work it together with the *crème fraîche*, beaten eggs, and flour. Fill the baked pastry with this filling.

Scatter pieces of bacon and small pieces of butter on the mixture. Bake for 20 minutes, then lower the heat to 350 degrees and bake for another 10 minutes, or until it is nicely puffed up and golden in color.

Serve hot or cold.

Serves 6 to 8.

Red Cabbage

- 1 red cabbage, weighing about ¾ pound
- 3 tablespoons unsalted butter
- 1 large onion, finely chopped
- 1 tablespoon salt
- 1 tablespoon dried thyme
- ¾ cup red wine

Slice red cabbage thinly, like sauerkraut. Wash in cold water.

Place butter in a *marmite* (see Glossary, page 262) or a heavy casserole. Add chopped onion and the cabbage. Add salt and pour over the red wine. Cover with a lid.

Simmer for 1 hour, stirring occasionally.

Serves 6.

Kafferkrautz — *Twisted Crown*

- ½ pound (1¼ cups) each all-purpose flour and cake flour
- 4 ounces (1 stick) unsalted butter, cut in thin slices
- 1 ¼-ounce (7-gram) package of yeast, dissolved in ¼ cup warm water
- 4 large eggs, beaten with ½ cup water
- ½ cup sugar
- ½ cup raisins

Sift the flours into a bowl and work in the butter with your fingers.

When the mixture resembles bread crumbs, stir in the yeast, eggs, and water.

Form a dough. Knead until smooth.

Add the sugar and raisins.

Let the dough rise in a warm place for 1 to 2 hours. Punch down.

Divide the dough in half, then form three 1-inch-thick ropes of dough from each half. Make two braids with three ropes of dough each.

Lay one braid in a circle on a baking sheet, spread with a little butter, and lay the second braid on top. Let rise again for about 1 hour.

Preheat the oven to 375 degrees.

Bake the bread for 45 minutes. [An instant-read thermometer, when plunged into the middle of the bread, should read 200 degrees.]

Serves 10 to 12.

Kougelhopf—*Almond Yeast Cake*

Kougelhopf or savarin molds are found in kitchenware stores.

    1   cup cake flour
    2   cups all-purpose flour
    9   ounces unsalted butter, thinly sliced
        Pinch salt
    ¾   cup sugar, plus 1 tablespoon
    3   large eggs, beaten

¼ cup kirsch
1 ¼-ounce (7-gram) package of yeast, dissolved in
¼ cup warm milk
¼ cup sliced almonds

Place the flours in a bowl and work in the butter with your fingers.

When the mixture resembles bread crumbs, add the salt, sugar, beaten eggs, kirsch, and yeast and milk.

Form a dough. Knead until smooth.

Butter a *kougelhopf* mold, place the sliced almonds in the bottom of the mold, and sprinkle sugar over the almonds. Fill the mold halfway with the dough and let it rise in a warm place for 1 to 2 hours, covered with a tea cloth.

Preheat the oven to 350 degrees. Bake 30 minutes.

Yield: 12 slices

Lorraine

People from Lorraine are generally good cooks. They make wonderful pastries. Many professional cooks come from this region. The recipes from Lorraine are nearly all delicious, because they have to please gourmands. It is a pleasure for me to give some lesser-known recipes here.

Foie Gras — *Goose or Duck Liver Terrine*

See Sources (page 265) for duck liver source.

- 1 goose or duck liver, weighing 1½ to 2 pounds
  Salt and freshly ground black pepper
- 2 black truffles, sliced [or 2 tablespoons black truffle puree (such as Salsa Tartufata by Urbani, see Sources, page 265) or 1 teaspoon white truffle oil]

Preheat the oven to 300 degrees.

[Bring the liver to room temperature. Carefully dig into it with your fingers and remove any stringy veins you may find.]

Cut the liver across in ¾-inch-thick slices. Sprinkle the slices of liver with salt and pepper and don't forget to include small pieces of truffle, black truffle puree, or truffle oil.

Place the sliced liver in a glass loaf or terrine pan measuring 5 inches wide, 3 inches deep, and 9 inches long. Cover the terrine with a lid or aluminum foil.

Put the terrine in a *bain-marie* (see Glossary, page 259) in the oven to cook for 40 minutes, or until the internal temperature of the liver reaches 120 degrees.

Stop the cooking by placing the terrine in a baking pan of cold water.

If a lot of fat has exuded, pour some off into a container and refrigerate. Use for cooking purposes, if you wish.

Refrigerate the foie gras. It will keep well refrigerated for 3 days.

Serve the liver at room temperature.

Serves 8.

Lorraine Meat Pie

1 pound each ground veal and pork
2 tablespoons olive oil
6 shallots, minced
2 cloves
   Salt and freshly ground black pepper
2 tablespoons fresh thyme [or 1 tablespoon dried thyme]
2 pounds puff pastry, bought or made (see page 143)
1 large egg yolk, mixed with 1 tablespoon water

Make a filling with the veal and pork, olive oil, shallots, cloves, salt and pepper, and thyme.

Prepare the pastry. Roll half of it out to a rectangle about 11 by 16 inches. Roll it up on the rolling pin and unroll onto a baking sheet.

Preheat the oven to 400 degrees.

Lay the filling on the pastry, leaving a 2-inch border. Brush the border with cold water.

Roll out the rest of the pastry to the same size and unroll over the meat. Press the edges together, trim the pastry and crimp the edges. Brush with an egg yolk mixed with water.

Make a chimney—a hole—in the center of the pastry to let the steam through. You can also make wide slashes 1½ inches apart in the pastry—to resemble a venetian blind.

Bake for 45 minutes.

Serves 8.

Quiche Lorraine

The quiche must become golden and set, but not overcooked. If the pastry underneath becomes soggy, the quiche is ruined. [For this reason, it is best to bake the pastry blind, that is bake it before adding the filling.]

1   recipe *pâté brisée* (see Glossary, *pâté brisée II*, page 263)
3   large eggs, beaten
¾   cup *crème fraîche* (see Glossary, page 260)
     Salt and freshly ground black pepper
6   slices bacon, cut in 1-inch pieces, cooked until crisp
½   cup Gruyère cheese, grated

Preheat the oven to 400 degrees.

Line a 9-inch tart tin with the pastry. Press aluminum foil on top of the pastry. Bake for 20 minutes, uncovering the pastry in the last 5 minutes. Do not turn off the oven.

Mix eggs, *crème fraîche*, salt and pepper, bacon, and Gruyère together. Pour this mixture into the baked pastry.

Bake for 20 minutes in a 400-degree oven, then lower the heat to 350 degrees and bake for another 10 minutes.

Serves 6.

Game Terrine

This terrine is best made with feathered game.

2	pheasants, boned and flesh sliced — save the scraps of meat for the filling and the carcass for stock
1	calf's foot, split by the butcher
1½	pounds each veal and pork, coarsely ground
6	sprigs parsley, chopped
5	shallots, minced
1	onion, chopped
2	truffles, finely sliced [or 2 tablespoons black truffle puree (such as Salsa Tartufata by Urbani, see Sources, page 265) or 1 teaspoon white truffle oil]
6	thick slices bacon, chopped
2	large eggs, beaten
	Fresh or dried thyme
	Pinch mace
	Pinch nutmeg

Start preparing a stock for jelly with the pheasant bones as soon as you have scraped all the flesh from the bones (see page 61). Add the split calf's foot to the stock.

Preheat the oven to 300 degrees.

Make a lightly beaten filling with scraps of leftover game, parsley, shallots, chopped onion, truffle peelings, bacon, eggs, thyme, mace, and nutmeg.

Layer the game, veal, pork, the filling, and finely sliced truffles in two 1-quart terrines or one 2-quart terrine [and cover with aluminum foil]. Bake for 2½ hours in a *bain-marie* (see Glossary, page 259). Pour the stock into the terrine.

When the terrine is cool, cover with a layer of melted lard or fat. If you want to preserve it for a long time, seal it hermetically with parchment paper and a layer of aluminum foil.

Refrigerate.

You can store these terrines from the opening of the hunting season until June. In winter, you can add some goose or duck liver to the mixture, which makes the terrine very delicate.

Serves 8 to 10.

Lorraine Noodles

[These noodles are to accompany meat or poultry dishes, or to serve simply on their own with butter.]

    4   large eggs
   2¼   cups all-purpose flour
        Unsalted butter

Mix eggs on a board with the flour to make a malleable dough.

Divide the dough in half and roll out as thin as possible. Cut into very fine strips. [Or use a manual spaghetti machine if you have one. Put a quarter of the dough in at number one and roll through. Keep adjusting the thickness until you reach number six. Then cut the noodles.

Sprinkle with flour or cornmeal.]

Preheat the broiler or heat the oven to 475 degrees.

Cook the noodles in boiling salted water for about 1 minute [until *al dente*].

Drain them, place them in a well-buttered casserole, and brown them under the broiler or the oven.

Serves 4 to 6.

Ramekin — A Cheese Soufflé

1   cup milk
3   tablespoons all-purpose flour
1   cup grated Gruyère cheese
    Salt and freshly ground black pepper
3   grinds nutmeg
3   large eggs, separated
    Unsalted butter

Bring the milk to a boil in a saucepan.

Place the flour in another saucepan. Slowly whisk the hot milk into the flour.

Place the mixture over low heat and cook, whisking constantly, until thickened—about 3 minutes.

Remove the pan from the fire, stir in the cheese, salt and pepper, 3 grinds of nutmeg, and egg yolks. Place the mixture in a bowl and let cool for 10 minutes.

Preheat the oven to 400 degrees.

[While the oven is heating up, place a baking sheet in it. When the soufflé dish is placed on top, the heat retained by the baking sheet will give an extra push to the souffle, and also prevent any overflow from arriving at the bottom of your oven.]

Butter the inside of an 8-cup soufflé dish, or 10 to 12 individual ½-cup ramekins. Beat the egg whites until stiff and fold in. Fill the soufflé dish or ramekins to ⅞ full.

Bake for 30 minutes. Individual ramekins take 10 to 15 minutes.

Serves 8 from the soufflé dish, or 10 to 12 in individual ramekins.

Lorraine Crepes

¾   cup all-purpose flour
2   large eggs
1   teaspoon olive oil
    Pinch salt
1   cup milk
    Vegetable oil

Mix together the flour, eggs, olive oil, salt, and milk to make a smooth batter.

Let the batter rest for an hour or two.

Make thin crepes over moderate heat. Pour a ladleful of the mixture into a heated 8-inch frying pan covered with a very thin film of oil; swirl the mixture to cover the bottom of the pan. When it starts to bubble, turn it and cook the other side.

Stack them and keep them warm. Eat them with salt.

Yield: 12 crepes.

Knepfen *or* Kneppes — *Gnocchi*

1 pound floury potatoes, baked, boiled, or steamed, and skinned
¾ cup all-purpose flour
3 large egg yolks
½ teaspoon salt
Unsalted butter
[¼ cup Parmesan cheese, grated or 1 cup tomato sauce (see page 49)]

Mash the potatoes and add the flour, egg yolks, and salt. Form into a dough.

Shape little 1-inch *knepfens* against the back of a fork. Throw them into boiling salted water.

Preheat the broiler or heat the oven to 375 degrees.

When the *knepfens* rise to the surface of the water, remove them with a slotted spoon and keep them warm in a buttered casserole. Add cheese or a tomato sauce and either place under the broiler until gratinéed or heat in the oven for 10 minutes.

Serves 4.

Matelote de *Metz* — *A Fish Stew Made with Red Wine*

1 10-ounce box pearl onions, peeled (see Glossary, page 263)
1 medium-size onion, sliced
1 bay leaf
1 clove
3 parsley sprigs

    1   shallot, sliced
        Salt and freshly ground black pepper
    2   cups fish stock (see page 59) or water
    1   pound each cod and haddock steaks, or 2 pounds
        cod only
    2   cups Côtes du Rhône red wine
  1½   tablespoons each unsalted butter and oil
    1   little ball of *beurre manie* (see Glossary, page 259)
6 to 8   bread slices fried in butter

In a large frying pan over moderate heat, brown the pearl onions in the butter and oil.

Add the sliced onions, bay leaf, clove, parsley sprigs, sliced shallot, salt and pepper, and water or stock. Simmer for 10 minutes.

Add the fish and red wine to cover. Simmer for 10 to 15 minutes.

Add a little ball of *beurre manie* and whisk in.

Remove the parsley and bayleaf; simmer for 2 to 3 minutes.

Pour into a preheated shallow bowl or casserole and garnish with slices of bread fried in butter.

Serves 6 to 8.

Financière *Cake from Nancy — Veal Soufflé*

[Have the sauce and garnishes ready before starting to prepare the soufflé.]

    2   cups milk
    3   cups bread crumbs
    3   tablespoons unsalted butter
    4   ounces ground veal

2 2-inch pieces beef marrow
Salt and freshly ground black pepper
1 teaspoon dried thyme
4 large eggs, separated
1 tablespoon *crème fraîche* (see Glossary, page 260)
1 recipe Crawfish Nantua Style (see page 145)
Garnish: 4 ounces each cooked mushrooms, sweetbreads, carp roe, and crawfish tails

Preheat the oven to 400 degrees.

Make a *bouillie* (see Glossary, page 259) by warming together
the milk, bread crumbs, and butter.

Mix the veal and beef marrow together and throw it into the
hot *bouillie*; add salt and pepper and the dried thyme.

Place all in a bowl. Add the egg yolks one by one, stirring after
each.

Beat egg whites until they are firm, and fold them into the mixture with the *crème fraîche*.

Butter an 8-cup soufflé dish or ten to twelve ½-cup ramekins.

[Place a baking sheet on a low rack in the oven. When the soufflé pan is placed on top, the heat retained by the baking sheet
will give an extra push to the soufflé, and also prevent any overflow from arriving at the bottom of your oven.]

Fill the soufflé dish or ramekins ⅞ full. Bake soufflé dish for 30
minutes. Ramekins will take 10 to 15 minutes.

Serve with crawfish and garnishes.

Serves 8 from the soufflé dish, or 10 to 12 in individual ramekins.

Lost Rice or Rice Pudding

[It is interesting to note that Pampille designates Carolina for the short grain rice she wants for this dessert.]

> ¾   cup Carolina rice, rinsed
> ⅓   cup sugar
> ½   vanilla bean, split
> ¼   teaspoon salt
> 4   cups milk

Preheat the oven to 300 degrees.

Place the rice in a casserole with the sugar and the vanilla bean. Add the salt and pour in milk to fill the casserole to three-quarters.

Bake, stirring occasionally, for 3 hours. Remove the skin that may form on the surface before serving.

Serves 4.

Kouglehopf —
Yeast Cake with Raisins

> 1   cup milk
> 4   ounces unsalted butter
> 1   ¼-ounce (7-gram) package yeast
> 3   cups all-purpose flour
> 3   eggs, beaten
>   Pinch salt
> ¾   cup sugar
> ½   cup raisins
>   Confectioner's sugar

Warm the milk, butter, and yeast in a saucepan.

Place the flour in a bowl with the eggs, salt, sugar, and raisins. Add the milk and yeast mixture. Stir it all together, beating for 10 to 15 minutes.

Place the dough in a well-buttered mold. It should fill a *kougelhopf* mold to one-third. Let the dough rise in a place where there are no drafts. Cover with a clean towel.

When the dough has risen, in about 2 hours, bake the *kougelhopf* in a 350-degree oven for ¾ hour.

Before serving, sift plenty of confectioner's sugar over the cake.

Serves 8 to 10.

Plombière —
Amaretti Soufflé

You can start preparing the base of the soufflé in the morning. [Buy store-bought *amaretti* — D. Lazzaroni & Co. make excellent *amaretti*.]

    2½ cups milk
    ½   vanilla bean, split lengthwise
    4   large eggs, separated
    ½   cup sugar
    7   tablespoons cornstarch
    ¾   cup (6 to 8) crushed *amaretti* or macaroons

Boil 2 cups of the milk with the vanilla bean; add the sugar.

Dissolve the cornstarch in remaining ½ cup cold milk.

Pour the dissolved cornstarch into the hot milk. Cook over a low fire and stir until it thickens slightly.

Take the pan off the fire and, stirring all the time, slowly add the egg yolks. When this is done, pour the mixture into a bowl and let it cool.

When it's time to eat, beat the egg whites until stiff. Fold the *amaretti* or macaroons into the egg whites. Fold this mixture into the first preparation.

Place the mixture in a buttered and sugared 8-cup soufflé dish, or 10 to 12 similarly prepared ½-cup ramekins.

Preheat the oven to 400 degrees.

[While the oven is heating up, place a baking sheet in it. When the soufflé pan is placed on top, the heat retained by the baking sheet will give an extra push to the soufflé, and also prevent any overflow from arriving at the bottom of your oven.]

Fill the soufflé pan or ramekins to ⅞ full.

Bake soufflé pan for 30 minutes. Individual ramekins will take 10 to 15 minutes.

Serves 8 from the soufflé dish, or 10 to 12 in individual ramekins.

Chocolate Cake

[You may glaze this cake with a chocolate glaze or simply powder with confectioner's sugar.]

9	ounces bittersweet chocolate, chopped
¾	cup milk
4	ounces (1 stick) unsalted butter
½	vanilla bean, split
⅔	cup sugar
½	cup cornstarch
1	cup ground almonds
6	large eggs, separated

[*Filling*
    1 jar apricot preserves, heated briefly and strained
Glaze
    8 ounces chocolate
    2 ounces unsalted butter
   ¼ cup milk
       or confectioner's sugar instead of glaze]

Preheat the oven to 350 degrees.

Butter two 9-inch cake pans and then line with parchment paper.

Over low heat, melt the chocolate in the milk with the vanilla bean.

Remove from the heat and add the butter and sugar.

Add the cornstarch, ground almonds, and egg yolks. Blend the mixture well.

Beat the egg whites until stiff and fold them in.

Divide the mixture between the two cake pans. Bake for 30 minutes. The inside of the cakes will remain moist.

When the cakes are cool, remove from the pans. Place one cake on a serving dish and spread with strained apricot preserves. Top with the second cake.

Melt the chocolate with the butter and milk. Stir until smooth and glaze the cake, or just sprinkle it with confectioner's sugar.

Serves 8 large or 16 small helpings.

Savoy and Dauphine

Trout Meunière

The river trout from Savoy and Dauphine are exquisite. You can't imagine the delicacy of their flesh unless you eat them on the spot. These trout are not shipped elsewhere. The trout we have in Paris, even though transported live in tanks, are unhappy trout. They no longer have the bounding torrent to swim in, and they don't seem to enjoy the final somersault into the frying pan.

    2   trout, weighing about 8 ounces each, gutted,
          trimmed of fins, and rinsed
          All-purpose flour
    4   tablespoons unsalted butter
          Salt

Coat both sides of the trout with flour.

Heat the butter in a frying pan over a moderate fire. Cook the trout, moving it every now and again so it won't stick to the pan. Do not overcook.

When it is cooked, place each trout on a hot plate. Sprinkle the trout with a little salt and pour over the butter that it was cooked in, which should be golden.

Serves 2.

Le Gratin Dauphinois — *Baked Scalloped Potatoes*

2½   pounds firm potatoes, such as red bliss or
     Yukon Gold, thinly sliced
1   large egg beaten
1   cup milk
4   ounces Gruyère cheese, grated
     Salt and freshly ground black pepper
2   tablespoons unsalted butter

Preheat the oven to 375 degrees.

Layer the sliced potatoes in a shallow casserole or gratin dish. Sprinkle each layer with pepper.

Beat the egg with the milk. Add the cheese and a pinch of salt.

Pour this mixture over the potatoes so that they all are moistened. Dot with small pieces of butter and bake for 1 hour.

Serves 5 to 6.

Matefaim —*A Large Buckwheat Pancake*

[This very large pancake may be eaten like bread or with a tomato sauce.]

> 1¼ cups buckwheat flour
> 5 large eggs, beaten
> ¾ cup water
>   Salt and freshly ground black pepper
> 3 tablespoons cognac
>   Olive oil

Place the buckwheat flour in a bowl. Gradually add the eggs and water and beat until smooth. Add a little salt and pepper, and the cognac.

Heat some good olive oil in a large, 12-inch frying pan over moderate heat. When the oil is hot, spoon in the batter to form a large pancake.

Once the pancake has become firm, turn it over with two wide spatulas so it cooks evenly on both sides.

Serves 8.

Limousin

Gâteau Limousin — Clafoutis — *Cherries Baked in Batter*

6	tablespoons all-purpose flour
6	tablespoons sugar
	Pinch salt
3	large eggs
1½	cups milk
¼	cup kirsch
1½	pounds beautiful black cherries, pitted if you wish
	Confectioner's sugar

Blend the dry ingredients.

Whisk the wet ingredients slowly into the dry so there are no lumps.

Preheat the oven to 400 degrees.

Butter an 8-cup shallow ovenproof serving dish or 12 individual ½-cup ramekins. Cover the bottom of an ovenproof dish or ramekins with the cherries, and pour the batter over.

Bake the serving dish for 35 to 40 minutes or the individual ramekins for 20 minutes.

Serve hot, sprinkled with confectioner's sugar.

Serves 12.

Las Farsaduras *(also known as* Farcidure*)* — *Cabbage Soup with Stuffed Cabbage Leaves*

    1   Cabbage Soup recipe (see page 19)
   1½   cups buckwheat flour or cornmeal
    ½   cup all-purpose flour
    ½   cup water
    ½   pound sorrel, finely chopped [or ½ pound
         mixed spinach and basil leaves, finely chopped]
    ½   bunch swiss chard, finely chopped
         Salt
    ¼   teaspoon *quatre épices* (see Glossary, page 263)
    3   thick slices bacon, finely chopped and cooked
         until crisp
    1   savoy cabbage, leaves striped off and blanched
         in boiling water for 5 minutes
         String

Mix the two flours together and add the water. Add the sorrel, swiss chard, salt, *quatre épices*, and bacon. Mix well.

Form a number of small balls about 1½ inches in diameter with this dough. Wrap them in cabbage leaves and tie them up with string.

The soup takes 40 minutes to cook over low heat; add the *farsaduras* (stuffed leaves) in the last 25 minutes.

Serve the soup with the stuffed cabbage leaves, vegetables, and salt pork on the side.

Serves 8.

Stuffed Mushrooms and Potatoes

This dish is a little heavy on the stomach if you abuse it, but it is exquisite.

    12 button mushrooms or *cèpes* (porcini) mushrooms,
        2½ inches in diameter
    12 small red bliss potatoes, steamed
     4 ounces each veal and pork, chopped
     ½ cup fresh bread crumbs
 1 to 2 cloves garlic, minced
         Salt and freshly ground black pepper
     2 tablespoons unsalted butter

Preheat the oven to 325 degrees.

Pull or cut out the stems from the mushrooms and rinse them. Cut the potatoes in half and make a small hollow in each half with a spoon.

Mix the chopped pork, veal, bread crumbs, garlic, and salt and pepper.

Fill the mushrooms and potatoes with the mixture.

Place them close together in an ovenproof earthenware or stoneware platter. Dot with pieces of butter, cover with buttered or oiled parchment paper, and bake for 40 minutes.

Take the paper off in the last 10 minutes.

Serves 4.

Lou Cassa-Musel — *Limousin Cake*

    6   tablespoons unsalted butter, softened
    ½   teaspoon salt
    ½   pound cottage cheese
   1½   cups cake flour
    ⅓   cup milk
    1   tablespoon sugar
    2   tablespoons sliced almonds

Preheat the oven to 350 degrees.

Mix the butter, salt, cottage cheese, flour, and milk together [in a food processor].

Butter an 8-inch tart tin and pour in the dough.

Sprinkle with sugar and almonds and bake for 1 hour.

Thus you have *cassa musel* or *cacha* (*casse-museau*), an excellent cake.

Serves 6.

Auvergne

There are few contrasts as striking as that between Auvergne and its inhabitants.

The beauty of Auvergne comes from the infinite variety of its graceful landscapes. Under skies that are always slightly hazy, a thousand springs keep the countryside fresh and cool all through the summer and into the autumn. From the heights — jagged crests that at sunset take on the aspect of proud fortifications — a view of bright pastures extends to the horizon. Mysterious lakes sleep in the craters of extinct volcanoes. There is no monotony to the rich plains, and it seems the swift brooks proliferate so as to provide for everything that needs water — the gardens, the clover fields, the great orchards.

And yet this region of ease, where life seems arrested in pastoral times, is the cradle of the most materialistic race of men, a race poor in artists and poets but well equipped for the struggle of existence. These descendants of the ancient Gauls could take as theirs the motto of William the Silent: "Hope is not required for enterprise, nor success for perseverance."

The contempt of the Auvergnat for the superfluous and the fashionable is part of his strength, but it also contributes to his legendary stinginess. So it is natural that when it comes to food, this practical man will look for "value" — to use a term he likes. Don't suggest fancy sauces or stuffings: what he wants is a feast of cabbage, bacon, and potatoes, which constitute the well-known *Soupe aux Choux*—Cabbage Soup. Here is the recipe for this country dish.

Cabbage Soup

You may also make Dried Bean Soup. Prepare it the same way as this Cabbage Soup, only place the beans in the cold water the night before and cook them in their soaking water.

    3   quarts cold water
    1   medium-size savoy cabbage, cored and cut into
        12 wedges or ½ pound dried white beans
    ¼   pound slab bacon, cut in 8 slices
    ½   pound each salt pork and ham, cut in 8 thick slices
    8   medium-size potatoes

Place the water in a *marmite* (see Glossary, page 262) and bring to a boil.

Throw in the cabbage, bacon, salt pork, ham, and potatoes. Cook for 45 minutes.

When the bacon is pink and transparent and the boiled cabbage has filled your house with the soup's strong smell, take out the bacon, salt pork, ham, potatoes, and most of the cabbage.

Taste the soup, and, if it is too salty, add some boiling water. Serve the soup over slices of whole wheat bread.

Serves 8.

Celeriac (Celery Root) Soup

This soup has a slightly wild taste that is not disagreeable. [Celeriac is available throughout the winter in fine produce stores.]

2	quarts cold water
1½	pounds celeriac—celery root—peeled and cubed
1¼	pounds potatoes, peeled and cubed
	Salt and freshly ground white pepper
1	cup milk
8	slices bread

Bring the water to a boil and throw in cubed celeriac and potatoes. Cook over moderate heat until they are tender, about 20 minutes.

Add the salt and pepper and the milk. Simmer for a few more minutes.

Pour the soup over slices of bread.

Serves 8.

Leg of Lamb with Potatoes

For a more festive dish than Cabbage Soup, the Auvergnats prepare Leg of Lamb with Potatoes. You can cook the potatoes in exactly the same manner without the leg of lamb, but then add more butter and bacon.

  4   pounds large red bliss potatoes or Yukon Gold
      potatoes, thinly sliced
  7   thick slices bacon, 3 of the slices cut in 1-inch pieces
  5   ounces unsalted butter, melted
  2   cloves garlic, minced
  2   cloves garlic, sliced lengthwise
      Salt and freshly ground black pepper
 ½   cup cold water
  1   leg of lamb

Preheat the oven to 375 degrees.

Use a large earthenware ovenproof dish, measuring 9 by 13 inches or thereabouts.

Fill the dish nearly to the top with thin slices of potatoes. Top with 3 slices of bacon cut in pieces, 4 ounces of butter, 2 minced cloves of garlic, salt and pepper, and cold water.

Insert thin slices of 2 cloves of garlic into the lamb, brush melted butter on it, and cover with 4 remaining slices bacon. Place the leg of lamb on top of the potatoes.

Take the dish to the baker. If you cook it in your oven the potatoes will not "melt" as well.

Bake for 1½ hours.

Serves 8.

Rouchides — *Potatoes with Bacon*

  3   thick slices bacon, cut in 1½-inch pieces
  1   pound firm, waxy kidney-shaped potatoes or
      Yukon Gold potatoes, peeled and thinly sliced
      Salt and freshly ground black pepper

Cook the pieces of bacon until crisp in an 8-inch frying pan over moderate heat. Remove the bacon pieces and put aside.

Add the potatoes to the bacon fat. Sprinkle with salt and pepper. From time to time, stir the potatoes so they cook evenly, about 20 minutes.

Add the bacon pieces.

Serve very hot and eat with whole wheat bread.

Serves 4.

As we are talking of potatoes, I must add the recipe for *Pachades,* a horribly indigestible dish. [!]

> 2 pounds potatoes, coarsely grated
> 2 eggs, beaten
>   Salt and freshly ground black pepper
> 2 tablespoons unsalted butter

Mix the potatoes with the eggs, and add salt and pepper.

Pour the mixture into a 12-inch frying pan in which you have melted the butter over moderate heat.

Cook until golden on both sides.

Serves 6.

Lamb Salmis — *Lamb Cooked with Red Wine*

The wine, which doesn't need to be a fine one, is special to Auvergnese cuisine. Nothing is better for the stomach, they believe, than very hot stock with some large glasses of wine added. After which they go straight to bed.

   8   pounds shoulder and shank of lamb or lamb chops,
       cut at least 1 inch thick
   4   medium-size onions, cut in 8 wedges each
   6   thick slices bacon, cut in 1-inch pieces
1½   tablespoons unsalted butter
   2   tablespoons olive oil
   3   tablespoons all-purpose flour
3½   cups red wine (see above)
   1   *bouquet garni,* (see Glossary, page 259)
       Salt and freshly ground black pepper
   ¼   cup cognac, optional

Bone out the lamb and save the bones. Trim the meat of fat and cut in 1-inch cubes — the butcher can do this for you.

Preheat the oven to 450 degrees.

Brown the bones in the oven, about 25 minutes.

In the meantime, brown the onions and bacon in the butter in a heavy casserole over moderate heat.

Brown the cubes of lamb in the olive oil, in batches, in a frying pan. Add them to the casserole as they brown.

Sprinkle the flour over the meat, stir and let brown.

Add the red wine to cover the meat, the *bouquet garni,* and salt and pepper. Also add the optional cognac.

[Add the browned bones — count them so you can remember how many to remove before serving.] Bring to a simmer and cover. Cook slowly. Check for doneness after 1¼ hours.

You can add some potatoes in the last 30 minutes, as in an ordinary stew, if you wish.

Serves 8.

Coq au Vin — *Chicken Braised in Red Wine*

I can highly recommend *Coq au Vin*. I don't know if this recipe is universally known. I only know of it from my cookbooks. [Chambertin is the best wine for this recipe; Côtes du Rhône will do.]

1	chicken cut in 9 pieces (see Glossary, page 260)
2	tablespoons unsalted butter
1	10-ounce box pearl onions, peeled (see Glossary, page 263)
4	slices bacon, cut in 1-inch pieces
1	tablespoon all-purpose flour
¾	cup chicken stock
1	*bouquet garni* (see Glossary, page 259)
2	cups red wine
	Salt and freshly ground black pepper
1	tablespoon red wine vinegar

Brown the chicken pieces in the butter in a frying pan over moderate heat. Place the chicken in a heavy casserole.

Brown the onions and bacon in the frying pan and add to the chicken.

Remove all but 2 tablespoons fat from the pan. Add flour and stir well.

Add the stock, *bouquet garni*, wine, salt and pepper. Stir and pour over the chicken. Cover and simmer for 30 minutes.

Add the red wine vinegar. Degrease the sauce before serving.

Serves 4.

Boudins — *Sausages with Apples*

Auvergne sausages, made from "*monsieur*" — the pig, as they ironically call him — do not in any way resemble those from a Parisien *charcutier*. This dish is a great combination and has a distinguished flavor. The sausages are beautifully perfumed with parsley, chervil, celery leaves, a glass of rum, and fennel seeds that have been dried in the oven, ground, and added at the end.

2 to 4   *boudins* [or other pork, veal, or chicken sausages]
       (1 or 2 sausages per person)
  4   tablespoons unsalted butter or olive oil
  2   peeled Reinette or Golden Delicious apples,
       each sliced in 16 slices
  4   teaspoons parsley, chopped
  4   teaspoons each chervil, tarragon, and celery leaves,
       chopped
  4   tablespoons rum
  2   teaspoons fennel seeds, crushed

Sauté the sausages in the fat; when they are cooked, push them to one side of the skillet and add the sliced apples.

When the apples are cooked, which will happen fairly quickly, serve them with the sausages on top.

Add the rest of the ingredients to the pan, cook briefly, and spoon over the top of the sausages.

Serves 2.

Mushrooms

Because of the abundance of mushroom sources, there isn't a single little wood in Auvergne that does not shelter a minuscule forest of mushrooms. There are the large *cèpes* (boletus or porcini) with strong firm flesh like venison, and the fragile chanterelles. Then there is a mushroom called "cinnamon," and another called "woodcock" that has sumptuous colors and looks as if it were poisonous.

This is a very simple way to prepare all mushrooms. You can look forward to having all the perfumes of a forest on your plate.

½   pound button mushrooms or *cèpes,* cleaned and sliced
2   tablespoons unsalted butter
     Salt and freshly ground black pepper
2   or more cloves garlic, sliced lengthwise

Cook the mushrooms with the butter in a frying pan over moderate heat. A large amount of moisture will accumulate, which you may spoon out or let evaporate. Add salt and pepper and as much garlic as you want.

Serves 2.

Tarts

Every year at Christmas my neighbor the baker prepares his oven especially for tarts. The procession of women with pastry boards on their heads begins early, each woman carrying one, two, or three tarts, depending on the wealth of her family. Some, made with love by unruffled housewives, have evenly latticed crusts with perfect edges. Other tarts bear the signature of the gossip, the muddleheaded, and the sour-tempered, who had to administer ten blows while making their pastry. Let's begin with the best.

La Tarte au Papa —*Papa's Tart*

First, make the "papa," which consists of a thick mixture of
flour and milk, flavored with vanilla or orange-flower water, to
which one or several egg yolks are added. This mixture, called
bouillie, must be cold when it is put in the tart.

½   pound puff pastry bought or made (see page 143)
2   cups milk
¼   cup all-purpose flour
3   tablespoons sugar
      Pinch salt
1   teaspoon vanilla essence, or ½ teaspoon orange-flower
      water
1   large egg
2   large egg yolks; 1 egg yolk mixed with 1 tablespoon
      water
3   tablespoons preserves such as gooseberry or apricot

Roll out the pastry and fit into an 8-inch tart pan. Use the leftover dough to make lattice strips. Refrigerate until you have
made the *bouillie*.

Gently heat 1 cup milk in a saucepan.

Whisk the other cup of cold milk into the flour, adding sugar
and salt.

Gradually add this mixture to the hot milk, whisking all the
time. When it comes to a simmer, continue to cook for 15 minutes over a very low fire, stirring occasionally.

Add the vanilla or orange-flower water.

Finally, add the egg and 1 yolk and stir until the *bouillie* has
thickened.

Strain it through a sieve into a bowl and place in the refrigerator until cold.

Preheat the oven to 400 degrees.

Lay the "papa" on the pastry and spread with the preserves on top. Arrange narrow strips on top in a lattice pattern. Fold over the edge and finish with a flat border ¾ of an inch wide.

Brush with the remaining egg yolk and water. Bake for 40 minutes.

Serves 6.

Le Cadet Mathieu —*An Apple Pie*

How to make a more current version of a tart.

    2 times recipe *pâté brisée* (see Glossary, page 262)
    7 apples (2¾ pounds), peeled, cored, and sliced, tossed
       with ¾ cup sugar
    1 large egg yolk, mixed with 1 tablespoon water

Preheat oven to 350 degrees.

Roll out just over half the pastry dough and fit into a 10-inch tart pan. Place the apple slices on the pastry. Wet the edges of the pastry with water.

Cover the top with the rest of pastry. Crimp the edges together. Make a hole in the center and other small holes here and there with a fork, so the steam can escape and a large cavern does not form under the pastry.

Glaze with the egg yolk and water.

Bake for 1 hour and 10 minutes.

Serves 8.

Acacia Fritters

I don't know the origin of these savory fritters, but they make a fine-tasting, pretty dish. The batter must be fairly thin.

[Acacias bloom in May and June. The flowers are formed in groups of blossoms like bunches of grapes. Try this recipe with zucchini blossoms also.]

    8   acacia blossoms [or 2 dozen zucchini blossoms]
    2   cups all-purpose flour
    ¾   cup water
    ¾   cup beer
        Pinch salt
    2   tablespoons olive oil
    2   large egg whites
        Deep-frying oil

Place the flour in a bowl and make a well in it. Add the water and beer slowly, whisking until the batter is smooth.

Add the salt and olive oil.

Let stand for 1 hour; beat the egg whites and fold them in before dipping the flowers in the batter.

Heat deep-frying oil to 365 degrees.

Fry in batches until golden. Drain on towels.

Serves 6 to 8.

Cheeses

I must also mention the end of the meal, when cheeses with very strong odors are presented. Even a small piece, very parsimoniously cut, will make you consume fifty times its volume in bread. Some Auvergne cheeses: Cantal, Saint Nectaire, Bleu d'Auvergne, Gaperon, Murol, Fourne d'Ambert.

Aveyron

Petites — *"Little Ones"* — *Stuffed Tripe Packages*

Serve this dish very hot. It is exquisite.

2½	pounds tripe, cut in eight 3-inch square pieces
8	3-inch square thin slices ham
3	carrots, peeled and finely chopped
1	large onion, finely chopped
3	celery stalks, finely chopped
½	bunch parsley, finely chopped
	Fines herbes (see Glossary, page 261)
	Salt and freshly ground black pepper
	String
8	½-inch-wide strips of fat back
7 or 8	lamb's feet or [½ calf's foot]
1	quart water

Lay the pieces of tripe out on a board. Place a piece of ham on top of each and a mixture of the finely chopped vegetables, *fines herbes*, and salt and pepper and form little rolled packages. Tie with white string.

Place the "little ones" in an earthenware pot with lamb's feet or calf's foot. Cover with water.

Simmer, covered for 2 to 2½ hours over a low fire.

Serves 4.

Foie Gras au Gratin — *Casseroled Goose or Duck Liver*

[See Sources, page 265, for duck liver.]

    1   goose or duck liver, weighing 1½ to 2 pounds
        Salt and freshly ground black pepper
  ½   cup bread crumbs
  ¾   cup chopped capers
  ¾   cup chopped cornichons or 1 black truffle, chopped [or 2 tablespoons black truffle puree such as Salsa Tartufata by Urbani, see Sources, page 265]

Preheat the oven to 300 degrees.

[Bring the liver to room temperature. Carefully dig into it with your fingers and remove any stringy veins you may find.] Sprinkle the inside and outside of the liver with salt and pepper.

Place the liver in a [glass loaf or] terrine pan [measuring 5 inches wide, 3 inches deep, and 9 inches long]. Sprinkle with bread crumbs.

Bake for 30 minutes [or until the internal temperature of the liver reaches 120 degrees. Stop the cooking by placing the terrine in a baking pan of cold water.

If a lot of fat has exuded, pour some off into a container and refrigerate. Use for cooking purposes, if you wish.

Refrigerate the foie gras. It will keep well refrigerated for 3 days.]

Serve the foie gras at room temperature with chopped capers and cornichons or chopped truffle.

Serves 8 to 10.

Chicken Fricassee Villefranche Style — with Ham and Onions

1 3½- to 4-pound chicken, cut in 9 pieces (see Glossary, page 260)
2 tablespoons unsalted butter
1 tablespoon olive oil or lard
¼ pound thinly sliced ham, cut in strips
1 onion, finely chopped
1 teaspoon all-purpose flour
1 cup chicken stock or water
   Salt and freshly ground black pepper
4 sprigs parsley
2 large egg yolks
1 tablespoon vinegar

Brown the chicken pieces in the butter and oil in a frying pan.

Remove the chicken pieces to a pot and replace with ham and finely chopped onion. Brown the onion gently, add the flour, then moisten with stock or water.

Pour the sauce over the chicken. Add salt and pepper and parsley sprigs.

Cook, covered, over low heat for 30 minutes.

In a bowl, blend the egg yolks with some of the sauce from the chicken and add the vinegar. Pour this liaison over the chicken. Mix in well by swirling the sauce in the pan and cook until the sauce has thickened to the consistency of cream.

Serves 4.

Shoulder of Lamb with Pistachios

Of course, the "pistachios" are really garlic cloves! If you try them once you must eat them again and again, or else you will shrivel away in despair.

[Have the butcher bone the lamb, roll and tie it with string.]

1	shoulder of lamb, boned, rolled, and tied with string
3	tablespoons unsalted butter or lard
1	onion, roughly chopped
2	tablespoons all-purpose flour
1	cup water
4	medium-size tomatoes, roughly chopped
20	or more cloves garlic
	Lemon juice (optional)

Brown the lamb shoulder in the butter or lard in a frying pan over moderate heat. When it is well browned, remove it from the pan and place it in a heavy casserole.

Brown the onion in the same fat.

Make a *roux* (see Glossary, page 263) in the pan using 2 table-spoons flour dissolved with 1 cup water.

Add the chopped tomatoes and cook briefly. Pour the sauce over the lamb.

Simmer for 1½ hours, covered.

Boil the cloves of garlic in water for 7 minutes and add to the sauce in the last 10 minutes; finish cooking the lamb with the sauce to perfume it a little. You may add some lemon juice, but it is not necessary.

Serves 4 to 6.

Hare en Cabessal

A *cabessal* is a small round padded pillow that women use to cushion their heads when they carry large pails of water from the fountains.

    1   hare [or large rabbit], skinned and gutted
        String
    4   tablespoons unsalted butter
    2   medium-size onions, sliced
    2   tablespoons all-purpose flour
    ½   cup red wine
    ½   cup chicken stock
        Salt and freshly ground black pepper
    4   sprigs parsley
    1   small bay leaf
    2   ounces pork rind, cut in strips
    1   slice bacon, finely chopped
    1   teaspoon parsley, finely chopped
    1   teaspoon onion, finely chopped
    2   teaspoons vinegar
    1   tablespoon olive oil

Form the hare or rabbit into a round, head to tail. Tie it in this uncomfortable position with string. Brown both sides in 2 tablespoons butter, then place in a large casserole into which the hare fits easily.

Separately, brown the onions in the rest of the butter over moderate heat. Make a *roux* (see Glossary, page 263) with the flour and moisten with red wine and stock. Stir well and pour this sauce over the hare.

Add salt and pepper, parsley sprigs, bay leaf, and pork rind.

Mix the bacon, chopped parsley, and onion together in a bowl. Stir vinegar and olive oil into this mixture and pour over the hare. Simmer for 2 hours or more. The rabbit will cook in an hour but you must be able to serve the hare with a spoon; a knife should not be necessary.

Before serving, place the hare on a platter. Pour the sauce over the hare.

Serves 6 to 8.

Oulade —*A Vegetable Soup*

Oulade is a soup made in an *oule*—an enamel pot. This is a very ordinary dish made by the peasants of Aveyron.
   [*Fritons* are scraps of pork.]

   1   recipe Cabbage Soup (page 19)
   1½   pounds *fritons* [or slab bacon]

Follow the instructions for Cabbage Soup, except before beginning to cook it, place a *fritonnière* or tin box pierced with small holes and containing *fritons* in the pot. If you don't have a *fritonnière*, a slice of slab bacon should do the trick. Use a strainer or cheesecloth to suspend the slab of bacon in the soup. You want the bacon to flavor the soup. Eat it separately.

You need about 2 hours to cook this soup. It should remain clear if it is made correctly.

Serves 8.

Mourtayrol —
Pot-au-Feu *with Beef, Chicken, and Ham*

Mourtayrol is a gala dish for Easter day.

> 3 pounds beef, top or bottom round or boneless chuck in 1 piece
> Cold water
> Raw vegetables as in recipe for *Pot-au-Feu* (see page 14)
> 1 5-pound chicken
> 2 pounds ham, in 1 piece
> 12 slices bread
> ½ teaspoon saffron

Place the beef in a large stockpot with water. Bring to a boil, skim it and add the vegetables as you would in an ordinary *pot-au-feu*.

Simmer for 4 hours. After 3 hours add the chicken and ham. When the soup is ready, fill a pot with slices of bread and pour the soup over them. Add the saffron. Cook over low heat for ½ hour until somewhat reduced.

Eat the *mourtayrol*—soup—first, then eat the beef, chicken, and ham later, to complete the feast.

Serves 12.

Confits d'Oies —*Preserved Goose*

You must get hold of some beautiful geese, stuffed with corn— real balls of fat. I will not write about how to kill them, carve them, or garner the livers. All these explanations are given in the recipe for *Les Confits Béarnaise* (see page 229).

Start this recipe 3 days at least before needed.

  2 or more geese
     Fat from the geese, livers reserved for foie gras recipes
     (see pages 166 and 200)
  1 cup water
     Salt and freshly ground black pepper
  6 cloves garlic, minced
     Leaves from 1 bunch fresh thyme
  2 pounds sausage meat

Cut the geese into pieces, pulling off all the excess fat that lies under the skin, and save the livers.

Render the fat with water—that is, cook it slowly—until all that remains is liquid fat and a few crisp pieces that you will remove. Refrigerate the fat.

[Rub the pieces of goose on both sides with salt, garlic, and thyme. Place on sheet pans and put them aside in the refrigerator for 24 hours.

Stuff the neck skins with sausage meat, sewing the ends closed.]

Melt the fat in a large pan. [Rub off the excess salt, garlic, and thyme from the goose pieces.]

Place the legs, cut in two, the wings, the necks stuffed with sausage, the breasts carefully removed from the carcass, the giblets, and the wing tips in the fat. Simmer for 2 hours, or longer if you are cooking a large amount, until you can easily pierce the goose with a thin needle or round toothpick.

The fat should become yellow and brilliant like oil. Place the preserved pieces in stoneware pots. Pour over enough fat to completely cover the pieces. Let them cool overnight. Fix a round of white paper to the top of each pot and then cover with the stoneware lids.

Refrigerate.

Serves 10 to 12.

Provence

Provence seems to me to have the best of all cuisines. This is not to insult the other regions, it's simply the truth. Everything you could wish for grows in this blessed countryside where the land is irrigated by water from the Rhône, Durance, and Sorgue rivers. Fruits and vegetables have exquisite flavor. This is the region, *par excellence*, for all fresh produce.

I can't think of anything more appetizing, on a very hot day, than sitting in the cool semi-darkness of a dining room with drawn Venetian shutters, and on the table finding black olives, Arles sausage, some beautiful tomatoes, a slice of watermelon that is a fountain of freshness, and a pyramid of small green figs baked by the sun. Later on, no doubt, we will not be able to resist an anchovy tart, roast lamb cooked on a spit with its perfectly browned meat, or a dish of artichokes with oil, their hearts so tender there is no need to remove the furry choke.

If you wish, you can feast yourself nearly exclusively on hors d'oeuvres and fruit. In this ephemeral air, on this happy terrain, there is no need to feel that you have to warm yourself with heavy meats or plates of lentils. The Midi is essentially a region of small, carefully simmered dishes.

I will give a certain number of Provençal recipes. I have chosen the most characteristic, and I regret that I can't give more—a whole book would not be enough to cover them all. Readers who wish to expand their knowledge of meridional dishes can find more in the book *La Cuisinière Provençale* by Reboul, Librairie Ruat, 54, rue du Paradis, Marseille. I have borrowed from this book [especially the *Bouillabaisse*, Mussels with Spinach, Shrimp Sauce, and Sauce *Poivrade*—among others]. These recipes are perfect and definitive. You have only to follow them step by step to be sure of succeeding. [This book is still sold in France. It is a classic.]

Aigo-Boulido —
A Soup Made with Boiled Water and Olive Oil

I have to admit that I don't like this oily soup. But it must possess marvelous properties, because people from Provence adore it and consider it a panacea against stomachache, migraine, homesickness, nostalgia, rheumatism, and so on.

    1   quart water
    1   tablespoon salt
    2   cloves garlic, crushed
    1   bay leaf
    2   tablespoons olive oil
    1   large egg yolk
    1   baguette, thinly sliced

Bring the first five ingredients in a saucepan to the boil. Simmer for ¼ hour.

Whisk an egg yolk in a soup tureen and add the soup gradually. Discard the garlic and bay leaf.

Serve hot with thinly sliced bread.

Serves 4.

Chickpea Soup and Chickpea Salad

Chickpeas used to be served only in the south of France. In Italy, and especially Spain, they consume a lot. The quality of Spanish chickpeas is excellent. They are large and floury and not difficult to cook. The chickpeas of the Midi are much smaller and harder; they resist softening and they have to be cooked in a special way. You can also cook the chickpeas after they have soaked all night in water with two handfuls of wood ash wrapped in a clean cloth or with a pinch of potash. In this case you have to change the cooking water halfway through cooking. But I assure you I have always had excellent results without adding ash or potash as long as I soak them overnight.

[Note: Start this recipe the day before you wish to serve it.]

- 1 pound spinach (optional), rinsed twice, stems removed
- 1 clove garlic
- 1 tablespoon all-purpose flour
- 1 pound dried chickpeas
- 3 leeks, trimmed of root ends and tough green leaves, cut lengthwise and rinsed, chopped
- 5 tablespoons olive oil
- 2 tablespoons vinegar
  Salt and freshly ground black pepper
- 2 tablespoons chives or shallots, finely chopped (optional)
  Croutons — small cubes of bread, fried in olive oil

Optional: Cook the spinach in 2 quarts of water for 5 minutes. Drain the spinach, saving the water. Eat the spinach on another occasion.

Soak the chickpeas overnight in the (spinach) water, adding the garlic and flour.

The next morning, after they have bathed in this lightly garlic-flavored (spinach) water, the chickpeas are tamed. Drain them. You can cook them without difficulty, as long as you start with *cold* water. If you plunge them in boiling water they will remain hard as marbles.

Cover the chickpeas by 4 inches of water in a pot. Place over moderate heat. When the water begins to boil, add 1 table-spoon salt.

After simmering for an hour, replace any water that has evaporated with boiling water. Boil until they are tender. The time will vary with the quality of the chickpeas—it is useless for me to give an exact cooking time. Usually 2½ hours is long enough.

When the chickpeas are cooked, strain them, saving the liquid.

Chickpea Soup

Place 4 cups of the cooked chickpeas back into the liquid; add 1 quart of water.

Fry the chopped leeks in 2 tablespoons olive oil. Add these to the chickpeas. Simmer for 30 minutes to 1 hour, when the chickpeas should be very soft.

Rub all through the medium mesh of a food mill. Serve with croutons.

Serves 6.

Chickpea Salad

Place the remaining chickpeas in a bowl and spoon over 3 tablespoons olive oil and 2 tablespoons red wine vinegar. Sprinkle with salt and pepper and toss. Add finely chopped chives or shallots if you wish.

Serves 4 to 5.

Bouillabaisse — *A Fish Soup*

Bouillabaisse, the triumph of Marseille, is really good only in Marseille. Don't try to eat it in Paris. Even in the best of restaurants they serve you, under the name of *bouillabaisse,* a fish soup that is thick and rich but with a flavor so strong you will quickly become disgusted. The plate of fish that is served afterwards consists almost exclusively of lobsters and some dull whiting. In Paris you could never have *rascasse, roucaou,* or John Dory for the very good reason that they *do not* travel well. Besides, the originality and the flavor of *bouillabaisse* lies in the variety of fish that it contains, and in their absolute freshness.

This admirable classic dish, so old that its origins are lost in the mists of time, is peculiarly Mediterranean. It is a regional dish for both rich and poor. In the narrow inlets where the wind sings in the pines, a poor fisherman can make as good a version as the most skillful Marseille chef, because *bouillabaisse* is poetry. To understand it, appreciate it, and, above all, to prepare it successfully, it is necessary to be born in Provence.

You can use, besides the *rascasse, roucaou,* and John Dory I have just spoken of, spiny lobster, weever, bass, crabs, and so on. Scale, clean, and slice the fish. Place them on two plates: one for the firm fish such as the lobster, *rascasse,* and sea robin; and the other for the soft fish such as bass, *roucaou,* John Dory, or whiting.

[Despite Pampille's admonitions you can make a pretty decent rendition of a *bouillabaisse* by replacing the above fish with rough equivalents. Vary the fish and shellfish with availability.]

½   cup olive oil
3   onions, finely chopped
4   cloves garlic, minced
2   tomatoes, peeled, seeded, and chopped
1   sprig thyme
½   fennel bulb, chopped
1   sprig parsley
1   bay leaf
1   1-inch-wide strip of orange zest
¾   pound firm fish [such as halibut fillet]
½   pound firm fish [such as monkfish]
    Boiling water
½   pound shrimp, cleaned
1   pound mussels, clams, or cockles, cleaned
    (see Glossary, page 262)
    Salt and freshly ground black pepper
½   teaspoon saffron
1   2-pound black sea bass, blackfish, rockfish, or
    red snapper, cut in ½-inch slices
    Lightly toasted slices of a baguette
1   recipe *Aioli* (see page 213)

Heat the olive oil in a heavy casserole or pot. Add the onions, garlic, tomatoes, thyme, fennel, parsley, bay leaf, and orange zest. Gently cook the vegetables for about 10 minutes, just to soften them.

Place the firm fish such as the halibut and monkfish on top and pour over some boiling water to barely cover. Add the shellfish.

Season with salt and pepper and saffron and bring to a boil. If the water does not come to a full boil quickly, the oil and water will not emulsify and the *bouillabaisse* will not be a success.

After 5 minutes of boiling, add the more tender fish slices, such as the sea bass or red snapper.

Boil for 5 more minutes, so the firm fish cooks for a total of *10 minutes.*

Pour the soup into a shallow earthenware casserole and serve with toast and *Aioli.*

Serves 8.

Aioli — *Garlic-Flavored Mayonnaise*

[If the emulsion breaks for any reason, break another egg yolk into a clean bowl and add the curdled mess slowly, beating continuously.]

3	cloves garlic
1	teaspoon coarse salt
2	large egg yolks
1½	cups olive oil
1	tablespoon lemon juice
1	very small pinch saffron diluted in 1 tablespoon warm water

Pound the garlic in a mortar with the salt. [Use the back of a spoon to crush the garlic in a bowl if you don't have a mortar.]

Add the egg yolks.

Whisk or beat in the oil drop by drop.

When you have a thick emulsion add the lemon juice and saffron.

[*Aioli* will serve as a very useful accompaniment to a variety of dishes. Use as butter!]

Yield: 1½ *cups.*

Bourride — *A Fish Soup*

You can make *bourride* with an assortment of fish or just one variety. I have eaten an excellent one in Marseille made exclusively with fresh sardines. A hungry stray dog that passed near our table in the open air stole half the dish with one swipe of his tongue. And then, because the *bourride* looked so good, we ate what the dog had left, with no regrets at all.

    1   large onion, chopped
    5   sprigs thyme
    1   small fennel bulb, chopped
    1   bay leaf
    1   1-inch-wide strip of orange zest
        Cold water
    ½   pound each [monkfish and halibut fillet, or whiting]
    2   1½-pound [black sea bass, red snapper, rockfish, or
        black fish] sliced in ½-inch slices
    ½   pound shrimp, peeled
    1   recipe *Aioli* (see page 213)
    8   slices bread, ½ inch thick, dried out in a warm oven
        and rubbed with garlic
    1   sliced baguette

Place the chopped onion, thyme, fennel, bay leaf, and strip of orange zest in a pot. Add the fish and pour warm water over to cover. Season with salt and pepper.

Bring to a boil. Simmer for 10 minutes. Turn off the heat.

In the meantime, place the bread in a shallow casserole or a soup tureen.

Stir ¼ cup *aioli* gradually into the fish stock, using a wooden spoon, over a low fire, *without letting it boil,* until it starts to thicken. Pour fish stock over the bread and serve the fish in a separate dish.

Guests may spread the *aioli* on slices of bread and dunk them in the soup.

Serves 8.

Poutargue des Martigues — *Caviar Made with Mullet Roe*

Poutargue is made with eggs from mullet roe gathered with a net. The fishermen of Martigues put them out in the sun to dry on a plank, with a few drops of olive oil. Another plank is then placed on top and weighted with large stones to press it down. The result is sticks of fish eggs that are as clear as amber when they are fresh, and that darken as they dry. But whether pale or dark brown, *poutargue* has a delicious taste that is very pronounced. Cut in small pieces and eaten with bread, like cheese, it is in my opinion even better than caviar. [Nowadays, it is nearly as expensive as caviar. To extend it and make it more palatable, mix it with the same amount of unsalted butter and serve with bread.]

Red Mullets Niçoise

Four cloves of garlic is not overdoing it, for red mullets absorb a lot. [Red mullets are sometimes available, imported from Europe, in local fish stores. They are wonderful fish.]

    4 cloves garlic, minced
    4 tablespoons parsley, finely chopped
    2 tablespoons tarragon
    3 tablespoons olive oil
  1½ pounds tomatoes, chopped
       Salt and freshly ground black pepper
    ½ cup dry white wine
    8 ½-pound red mullets [(imported from the
       Mediterranean), trout, mackerel, or porgies]
       All-purpose flour

Preheat the oven to 400 degrees.

Cook the garlic, parsley, and tarragon over a low fire with the
olive oil.

After a few minutes, when the mixture has taken on color,
throw in the chopped tomatoes. Season with salt and pepper.
Simmer the sauce for 30 minutes, adding the wine in the last 10
minutes.

Grease a long oven dish *very lightly*, with olive oil. Dip the red
mullets in flour and lay them in the dish.

Rub the garlic and tomatoes through a food mill over the fish.
Bake for 20 minutes.

Serve immediately.

Serves 8.

Mussels with Spinach

    2 tablespoons olive oil
    2 medium-size onions, finely chopped
    2 pounds spinach, rinsed twice, stems removed
    2 tablespoons all-purpose flour dissolved in ½ cup milk

½ cup milk
  Salt and freshly ground black pepper
1 clove garlic, minced
1 carrot, finely chopped
1 small onion, finely chopped
1 bay leaf
2 parsley sprigs
2 cups dry white wine
4 pounds mussels, cleaned (see Glossary, page 262)
1 cup bread crumbs
1 teaspoon olive oil

Preheat the broiler.

In a large pan heat the olive oil and brown 1 chopped onion.

Add the spinach; stir and cook for 5 minutes until it has wilted. Drain and, when cool enough, squeeze dry and chop finely.

Place the spinach in a pan and add the flour and milk mixture — heat over moderate heat and stir.

Add the other ½ cup milk, salt and pepper, and garlic. Simmer until the mixture slightly thickens. Put aside.

Place the chopped carrot, onion, bay leaf, parsley, and wine in a large pan. Add the mussels and cook, covered, for 5 minutes, when they should all open. Discard any that do not open.

Remove the opened mussels to a bowl. Take them out of their shells — keeping the best-looking shells. Cook the mussel juices over moderate to high heat until reduced by half.

Put 2 mussels in each shell. Fill up the shells with a small spoonful of the spinach mixture.

Sprinkle the mussels with bread crumbs, moisten with a few drops of olive oil, and place them under the broiler until they brown slightly.

Serves 4.

Eggplant Provençale

It is recommended that you prepare this dish the day before needed, for it will be even better reheated the next day.

3   tablespoons olive oil
4   pounds plum tomatoes, seeded and finely chopped
3   1½-pound eggplants, sliced lengthwise in ½-inch, shoe-sole-shaped slices
1   bunch chervil (substitute ½ bunch tarragon if unavailable, or parsley if neither is available), chopped
4   cloves garlic, minced
    Olive oil for brushing the eggplant
    Salt and freshly ground black pepper

Preheat the oven to 450 degrees.

Heat 3 tablespoons oil in a heavy pan over moderate heat. Place the tomatoes, garlic, and chervil in the pan.

Stir well and wait for it to boil. Lower the heat and simmer for 1 hour.

Score both sides of the eggplant slices crosswise with the point of a knife.

Brush the eggplant slices with olive oil and bake in batches in the oven on baking or cookie sheets until golden. Remove and lower the oven heat to 400 degrees.

In a large, long earthenware platter or shallow casserole, arrange a layer of eggplant, then a layer of tomatoes, a layer of eggplant, and so on, finishing with a layer of tomatoes.

Bake the dish for 30 to 40 minutes, until bubbling hot.

Serves 8.

Artichokes Provençale

You can eat baby artichokes whole, even the choke and all of the leaves. Drink water when you eat them, because wine will taste bitter; the water will take on a sweet delicious taste.

18 tender baby artichokes
    Juice of 1 lemon
    Olive oil
    Salt and freshly ground black pepper
    Cold water
2 tablespoons mint or thyme, finely chopped (optional)

Pull off the outer leaves and trim the tips of the inner leaves of the artichokes with scissors or a knife. Trim the stalk ends. Rub the artichokes with lemon juice to keep them from darkening.

Sprinkle the artichokes with olive oil and put quite a lot of salt and pepper between the leaves.

Pour 1 tablespoon olive oil on the bottom of a saucepan, and stand the artichokes up in it. Add cold water to cover. The artichokes should fit closely in the saucepan.

Place the pan over a high fire so that the water boils and evaporates quickly. In 20 to 30 minutes the artichokes should be cooked and only a little olive oil should remain in the pan.

Place your artichokes on a hot platter and pour over the remaining oil.

Serves 6.

Small Birds

Everyone in Provence likes small birds. This wonderful game, rarely cooked nowadays, is hunted in September in the hills of Provence, although some argue that those from the marshes are better. These poor small birds are so good to eat because they have fed on wild bay leaves and grains perfumed by the air of the mountains. They taste exquisite—of wild thyme and mint. You don't need to season them.

Here is the best way to prepare them:

Feather and gut the birds, leaving them whole with head and feet on. String them by the half dozen on *brochette* sticks, separating each bird from the other with a small square of larding bacon.

Roast them in front of a fire of vine shoots. Fifteen minutes is all it will take.

Serve them, basted with their own juices, smoking hot on the *brochette* sticks.

Some people haven't the patience to carve the birds. They make a mouthful of the heads, crunching down on the bones. This is not a bad idea.

6 birds (1 brochette stick) serves 1

Stuffed Sardines

This is an excellent hors d'oeuvre.

- 8 fresh fat sardines, heads off and gutted, split through the stomachs lengthwise, backbones removed, and opened up flat
- 4 tablespoons unsalted butter, softened

   4   tablespoons parsley, finely chopped
       Salt and freshly ground black pepper
   1   lemon

Spread a mixture of equal parts butter and parsley on all the sardines. Stick one buttered sardine against another.

Grill, fry, or broil these "sandwiches."

Garnish with lemon wedges.

Yield: 4 "sandwiches" (hors d'oeuvre for 4).

Languedoc

Preserved or Fresh Cèpes Nîmoise

These mushrooms are only in season from summer through November. [Not often available in the United States, we may use dried *cèpes*, which taste good but can't compare with the fresh.]

- ¼ cup olive oil
- 1 pound fairly large *cèpes*—if they are fresh, clean them with a white cloth [or 5 ounces dried—rehydrated in warm water for 1 hour, then drained]
  Salt and freshly ground black pepper
- 4 cloves garlic, minced
- ⅓ cup parsley, finely chopped

Heat the oil and cook the *cèpes* in a pan over moderate heat until they start to color. Add salt and pepper, garlic, and parsley. Stir once or twice.

Seal the pan hermetically with parchment paper and a lid and simmer over a very low fire for 20 minutes.

Serves 4.

Stuffed Tomatoes —
With Meat or Bread Crumb Stuffing

It is very important to cook dishes with oil *slowly*. This is the secret of the meridional cuisine.

    4   beautiful ripe medium-size tomatoes

Meat filling
- 1 cup cooked meat, finely chopped (such as the beef from *Pot-au-Feu*, page 14)
- 3 tablespoons parsley, finely chopped
- 1 clove garlic, minced
     Salt and freshly ground black pepper

Bread crumb filling
- 1 cup fresh bread crumbs
- ¼ cup milk
     Salt and freshly ground black pepper
- 6 tablespoons parsley, finely chopped
- 2 large hard-cooked egg yolks, crumbled
- 1 large clove garlic, minced

- 1 tablespoon olive oil
- ¼ cup cold water

Preheat the oven to 300 degrees.

Cut a hole in the top of each tomato and hollow them out, discarding their seeds. Drain upside down on a rack for 30 minutes.

Prepare either filling by mixing the ingredients in a bowl. Stuff the tomatoes.

Place olive oil in the bottom of an oven dish and place the stuffed tomatoes in it. Add the water.

Bake for 25 minutes.

Serves 4.

Snails Nîmoise

Take large gray snails from the vineyard that have fasted in a dry place for 20 days, at least. Before cooking, pull off the little veil that covers them. Let them disgorge in water that has a lot of vinegar and salt added to it. They foam and spit and you have to change the water often until they stop foaming.

Go through them one by one and discard any rotten snails, for they will affect the taste of the others.

Create a *court-bouillon* (see Glossary, page 260) with water, salt and pepper, clove, garlic, onion, carrot, thyme, bay leaf, and tarragon.

Add the snails and simmer for 2 to 3 hours, until they have become tender.

Make a sauce composed of finely chopped parsley, a clove garlic, and olive oil; cook over low heat. Make enough of this sauce so that the shelled snails, placed in it for ½ hour before serving, become impregnated with the perfume. You can also add small bits of cooked bacon to the sauce, if you are not eating the snails on Friday.

It goes without saying that you have to replace each snail inside its shell before serving.

Alternative Recipe

2 tablespoons parsley, finely chopped
4 cloves garlic, minced

6 tablespoons unsalted butter, softened or olive oil
Pinch salt
12 snails and their shells (bought from specialty stores)

Preheat oven to 400 degrees.

Mix together parsley, garlic, butter or oil, and salt.

Place 1 snail in each shell. Fill with the flavored butter or oil.
Place 6 snails in each of two oven proof snail dishes, with small
dents to hold each snail, or in a dish filled halfway with coarse
salt in which the snail shells can be placed upright.
Bake for 7 minutes or until bubbling hot.

Serves 2.

Lamb Carbonnade

In the evenings, the good people of Nîmes set out from their
homes to fetch their cooked lamb, from the baker, which they
consume with gusto, washing it down with fresh local wine.
They take the dish to the baker in time to use the hot oven after
the bread has been baked. This dish can cook without anyone
watching it. The baker's boy will take it out when it is cooked.

½ leg of lamb, boned and tied in a round
Olive oil
Salt
3 pounds small potatoes, peeled

Preheat oven to 400 degrees.

Brush the lamb with olive oil and sprinkle with salt. Place it in
an earthenware dish, surrounded with potatoes. Sprinkle the
potatoes with olive oil and bake for 1½ hours.

Serves 4.

Béarn

Béarn is a happy region. Perhaps because of this, one doesn't yearn for it in the same way as one yearns for Brittany or Provence, which speak to stronger passions. But here more than anywhere else it is easier to understand the joy of being free and strong—an earthly joy that is perhaps a bit selfish, but that takes on a remarkable reality on Béarnaise soil. Even the weakest souls feel this joy when they are served *Garbure*— Cabbage Soup.

To truly appreciate *Garbure,* you should eat it in the company of Pierre Lasserre at the inn at Betharram, halfway between Lourdes and Pau. There you are within the sound of the ever-flowing, clear green waters of the Gave, overlooking charming rocks that while not all evoking tragedy, add force and balance to this blissful landscape.

This regional dish, which forms the basis of Béarnaise peasant cooking, varies in ingredients according to the season. Similarly, as the quality of the cabbage changes, so does the cooking time. In the winter the cabbages are harder, mounted on stems—these are the green or Cavalier cabbages. They have large leaves and are not quite round. You have to throw out the first water that they are cooked in, after it comes to a boil, and replace it with fresh water. These green cabbages take at least 2 hours to cook.

In the spring, use small round cabbages with curly crackling leaves—savoy cabbages. These cabbages must cook for 1 hour, or maybe less if they have just been picked, or if they jump, still alive, directly from the bottom of the garden into the pot.

Finally, in summer there are white cabbages that are not very good and must be cooked quickly; if not they will taste awful.

Nothing is better or healthier and, although this might seem paradoxical, nothing is more digestible than *Garbure* when it is well prepared and eaten in Béarn.

Let me add that a good bottle of Jurançon is the happy indispensable accompaniment to *Garbure*. This celebrated light, red, fruity wine can be treacherous, because it goes to your head immediately. You will be a happy drunk, making mistakes in the French language and not being able to conjugate verbs. It will make you say *finoir* for *finir* and *recevir* instead of *recevoir*. But at least it doesn't make everyone crazy, like the terrible Burgundies.

Garbure — *Cabbage Soup*

The addition of a red chili pepper is particular to Béarn—it is long and thin and grows in the summer. It is left to redden on the vine until autumn and is a superior replacement for pepper. *Garbure* has to be a thick soup, so thick a spoon can stand up in it. Therefore there must be lots of cabbage; the beans or potatoes are only there to give more consistency to the broth. In spring you can replace the beans with fresh shelled fava beans and baby green peas.

½ pound dried, small, round, white beans or 2 pounds potatoes, peeled and cubed
1 fresh or dried red chili pepper [or a jalapeno pepper]
1 *bouquet garni* (see Glossary, page 259)
3½ quarts water
1½ pounds preserved goose (page 229) or smoked pork butt
1 savoy cabbage, cored and cut in 12 wedges
2 medium-size white turnips, peeled and diced

First cook the beans or potatoes with the chili pepper and the *bouquet garni* in water. Simmer the beans for 1 hour or the potatoes for 25 minutes. If using beans, add the preserved goose or pork butt and simmer for another hour. If using potatoes, remove them before cooking the meat for 1 hour. Set aside the chili pepper, the *bouquet garni,* and the preserved goose or pork butt.

Rub the beans or potatoes and their water through the medium mesh of a good mill twice.

Put everything back in the same pot and add the cabbage wedges and diced turnips. Bring to a boil and cook for 20 to 30 minutes more, depending on whether you like your cabbage firm or soft.

There are two ways to serve *Garbure*:

The first way is to put slices of bread into the soup tureen and pour the contents of the pot over them.

The second, and more common, way is to pour the soup without bread into the soup tureen, and to serve *Bouillie* (see below) alongside.

Eat the preserved goose or pork separately, surrounded with large boiled potatoes.

Serves 8.

Bouillie — *To Be Served with* Garbure

[I find this recipe quite unnecessary to serve with *Garbure,* which is a delicious creamy vegetable soup by itself. But here is the method.]

    1 baguette
    4 cups broth from *Garbure*

Slice a stale baguette.

Place these slices in a pot, moistening them with 2 cups of broth from the soup.

As the bread soaks up the liquid, slowly add 2 more cups of broth and place over a low fire.

Simmer for approximately 20 minutes. The *bouillie* must be thick without becoming solid; serve it in a small tureen alongside the *Garbure*.

Les Confit Béarnaise —*Preserved Goose or Duck*

Here is the recipe for the marvelous preserved goose that is a great boon to farsighted housewives throughout the southwest during the winter. They prepare it every year at the end of autumn. It is an important process that demands a great deal of care.

1   9-pound goose or 2 ducks
6   cloves garlic, minced
½   bunch fresh thyme, chopped
4   tablespoons coarse salt

Confit de Canard—preserved duck—is prepared exactly the same way as the goose, except that duck does not furnish enough fat, so you have to cook it with added pork fat. Béarnaise cooks say that the goose "*se couvre,*" which means that it furnishes enough fat to fill the jar of wings, breasts, and thighs.

There are two ways to kill the fattened geese—force fed with corn for a period of 15 to 20 days prior to being preserved.

1. Simply bleed the geese. Kill them and hang them, head down, to bleed so that not a single

drop of blood remains in the body; if this is not
done, the liver will not be lily-white.

2. Break the spinal cord. To do so, hold the goose
    by the feet with its head down, place a large stick
    on its neck, step on the stick with one foot to the
    right and one to the left and yank up the goose
    feet. Death is instantaneous because this breaks
    the spine. Immediately hang the goose with its
    head down, so that all the blood will drain
    through the neck (country folk consider this a
    very tasty part), and the goose's flesh will be per-
    fectly white.

Pluck the goose. This is a delicate operation since the skin is
very tender, and a well-plucked goose must have skin that is ab-
solutely white and smooth, without any tears in it.

Cut open the goose (leaving the carcass whole as when boning
a chicken). Detach the neck, the head, the feet, and the wing
tips from the body. Cut off the legs, wings, and breasts from
the carcass. Set these pieces aside on a large platter—we will
come back to them later.

Remove the liver—let's hope you have the pleasure of finding it
large and white. Soak it in cold water in order to remove all remaining traces of blood, changing the water as necessary. Continue to do this overnight. When the liver is completely white,
place it on a folded napkin. It is now ready to be cooked and
eaten immediately or preserved (pages 166 and 200).

You will also remove the intestines, and, before throwing out
the carcass, cut off all the fatty skin and pull out the fat from
the interior of the carcass. Render the fat and skin with ½ cup
water in a saucepan over moderate to low heat until very few
solid pieces are left. The rest should be pure liquid fat. Strain,
pour into a jar and refrigerate.

Let's return to the goose and refer to recipe for *Confits d'Oies,* (page 205) in the Aveyron region.

Toss the garlic and thyme with coarse salt. Spread the mixture over the goose wings, breasts, legs, wing tips, necks, feet, and giblets. Lay the parts skin-side down on a shallow dish or platter [cover with plastic wrap] and refrigerate for 3 days.

After 3 days, melt the fat that you've kept in a jar in a large pot over *a very low fire.* Add all the pieces of goose and simmer for about 2 hours. The necks and gizzards will be cooked first, then the thighs and wings and breasts. To test whether they are done, pierce them with a toothpick from time to time. When the juice runs clear, they are cooked.

Place the wings, breasts, and thighs in a stoneware jar. When they are nearly or completely cold and the fat is tepid, pour the fat over the pieces, covering them well. Let the fat get solid; it should be hard and white.

Cover the fat with a round of white paper slightly moistened on the bottom and dipped in salt. Then cover the jar with another piece of paper and tie it well with string, like jam jars.

The necks and gizzards should be placed separately in another jar, because they don't last as well as the wings and thighs. Eat them first.

The salted wing tips, feet, and usually the giblets are served within 8 days of making the preserved goose, because they give an excellent taste to *Garbure* (see page 227).

Of course you must keep the preserved goose in a cool place.

Serves 8. Yield: 2 wings, 2 breasts, and 2 legs, each of which can be cut in two pieces.

Piperade —*A Tomato Sauce To Pour Over Fried Eggs*

This delicious dish, when well made, should be served with eggs fried in oil—don't use butter! This sauce has to be cooked a *long time* to be good.

  1 medium-size onion, finely chopped
  2 tablespoons olive oil
  2 pounds plum tomatoes, seeded and chopped
  2 long green (Italian) peppers, finely chopped
  1 tablespoon olive oil or goose or pork fat
     Salt

Fry the chopped onion in a frying pan until soft over moderate heat, then add the tomatoes. Stir from time to time.

In another frying pan, fry the green peppers in olive oil or goose or pork fat. When they have taken on color, drain them from the fat and add them to the tomatoes.

Cook the *Piperade* over a low fire for ¾ to 1 hour. Lightly season with salt.

Serve with fried eggs.

Serves 6.

Gascony
and the Bordelaise Region

Daube

A Gascon *daube* is perhaps the best of all the *daubes,* when it is a success. [*Daube* is a long-cooked braised dish of meat and red wine, first cooked on top of the stove, then finished in the oven.]

4	cloves garlic, slivered
3 to 4	pounds stewing beef in 1 piece, such as boneless chuck
1	slice of pork rind
½	pound salt pork or pork belly, cut in 2-inch-long, thin strips
1½	cups red wine
¾	cup water

  3 carrots, peeled and sliced
  1 clove
  1 *bouquet garni* (see Glossary, page 259)
     Salt and freshly ground black pepper

Preheat the oven to 300 degrees.

Insert slivers of garlic into the meat as you would lard a piece of meat — that is, not sparingly.

Place the meat in a heavy casserole on top of a slice of pork rind and a piece of salt pork that has been cut in lardons. Add red wine and water, to nearly cover the meat. Add the carrots, clove, *bouquet garni*, and salt and pepper.

Bring to a boil on top of the stove and then transfer to the oven, covered. Cook for 2 to 3 hours, until a piece of the beef melts in your mouth. Test for tenderness after 2 hours.

Degrease the sauce and strain it if you want before serving.

Serves 6 to 8.

Grape Harvester's Soup

Eat this soup in the middle of the vineyards after a riotous morning's work in the fresh air of the Gironde river. This soup is worth more than any of the fancy dishes on menus at refined restaurants.

      2 cloves garlic, slivered lengthwise
 3 to 4 pounds stewing beef in 1 piece,
            such as boneless chuck
            Cold water
     ¼ pound carrots, peeled and sliced
      2 medium-size onions, sliced

1 savoy cabbage, cored and sliced
3 tablespoons olive oil
2 celery stalks, chopped
2 leeks, trimmed of root ends and tough green leaves,
    cut lengthwise and rinsed, chopped
2 medium-size white turnips, peeled and chopped
2 tablespoons all-purpose flour
1 pound plum tomatoes, seeded and chopped
    Salt and freshly ground black pepper
1 *bouquet garni* (see Glossary, page 259)

Insert slivers of garlic into the meat. Place in a large pot and add water to cover and bring to a boil.

Skim and add carrots, onions, and cabbage. Simmer.

In the meantime, brown the celery, leeks, and turnips in the olive oil in a pan over moderate heat.

Sprinkle with the flour and stir well. Add to the pot.

Place the tomatoes in a separate saucepan, crush them and cook over moderate heat. Season them well with salt and pepper and a *bouquet garni.*

After 20 minutes, rub them through a food mill into the pot with the meat and vegetables.

Simmer for another 2 hours before serving. Taste for tenderness and cook longer if necessary.

Serves 6 to 8.

Tourin Bordelaise — *Onion Soup*

2 pounds onions, sliced
2 tablespoons unsalted butter
1 tablespoon olive oil

1   clove garlic
1   quart water
½   teaspoon salt
    Freshly ground black pepper
3   large egg yolks, beaten
1   teaspoon red wine vinegar
1   stale baguette, sliced

In a heavy casserole, brown the onions in the butter and oil over a low fire.

Stir often with a wooden spoon, to ensure even cooking.

When the onions have wilted and are browning, add the garlic, water, salt, and pepper. Bring to a boil and let boil for 10 minutes.

In the meantime, mix the egg yolks, vinegar, and ¾ cup of the hot soup together. Pour this into the hot *tourin*—onion soup—stirring constantly and taking care it does not boil again.

Place rounds of stale bread in the soup tureen and pour the *tourin* over it.

Serves 8.

Landais Omelet

[York ham is the French name for boiled ham.]

1   round loaf bread, cut in four ½-inch-thick slices,
    crusts removed, cut in 2½-inch rounds
    Unsalted butter
    Salt and freshly ground black pepper
8   large eggs
4   slices York [boiled] ham, cut in thin strips

Preheat the oven to 450 degrees.

Fry the rounds of bread in butter over moderate heat, until they are golden.

Use a shallow ovenproof dish and butter it copiously. Sprinkle with salt and pepper and place the toast on the butter.

Break the eggs into a bowl. Add salt and pepper and ham. Beat the mixture and pour it into the dish with the bread. Spread the ham out evenly.

Bake for 8 to 10 minutes. You want the omelet to be a little soft.

Serve right away while the eggs are puffed up and looking delicious.

Serves 4.

Bouchées Pauillacaises — *Potato Balls with Meat Filling*

[It is interesting to note that Pampille used a meat extract called Liebig on occasion.]

> 2 pounds [Yukon Gold] potatoes, peeled, cut in 1-inch cubes
> 2 tablespoons unsalted butter
> ½ cup milk
> Salt and freshly ground black pepper
> Freshly ground nutmeg
> 4 large eggs, beaten
> 1 cup fresh bread crumbs
> Deep-frying vegetable oil

Meat filling
> 1 tablespoon unsalted butter or olive oil
> 2 shallots, minced

   1   onion, finely chopped
   1   tablespoon all-purpose flour
  ¾   cup beef stock or ½ beef stock cube dissolved in
       ¾ cup hot water
       Salt and freshly ground black pepper
   1   cup roast or braised leftover meat such as veal, beef, lamb, or chicken, diced

Steam the potatoes until soft.

Preheat the oven to 300 degrees.

Make the meat filling: Melt butter or oil in a saucepan. Add the shallots and onion and sauté over a low fire. Add the flour and let brown. Moisten with the beef stock. Season with salt and pepper and let reduce over moderate heat. Stir in the diced meat. Set the mixture aside.

Rub the potatoes through a ricer or food mill into a pan. Add the butter and milk. Season with salt, pepper, and nutmeg.

Beat the pureed potatoes well over low heat for 3 to 5 minutes until they are very dry and thick. Add 2 beaten eggs. Beat again. Your puree should be very thick. Remove from the fire and cool.

Make balls the size of an egg with the potato puree. Flatten them lightly and make an indentation in the middle of each.

Heat oil to 365 degrees. Dip the balls of potato puree in beaten egg and then in bread crumbs. Fry them in the hot oil, in batches, until golden, about 2 minutes. Drain on towels and put aside.

Pile the diced meat filling in the middle of each *bouchée* like a dome and place in an ovenproof dish. Heat in the oven for 15 minutes.

Serve hot.

Serves 8.

Manchons de Boeuf—
Beef Bundles Filled With Cèpes

If fresh *cèpes* are not available, use dried *cèpes* or button mushrooms.

    1½ pounds beef, bottom, top round, boneless chuck,
        or eye round, in 1 piece
     3 ounces [button mushrooms or] *cèpes* or 1 ounce dried
        cèpes, diced
     3 ounces Bayonne ham [or prosciutto] sliced ¼ inch
        thick, diced
     1 tablespoon olive oil or goose fat
     1 clove garlic, minced
     3 tablespoons parsley, finely chopped
     ¾ cup fresh bread crumbs
        Salt and freshly ground black pepper
        String
     1 large onion, finely sliced
     4 carrots, peeled and chopped
     1 *bouquet garni* (see Glossary, page 259)
     ¾ cup dry white wine
     ¾ cup beef stock [or half a beef stock cube dissolved in
        ¾ cup water]

Preheat the oven to 350 degrees.

Cut the meat into 8 pieces. Pound them and shape into more or less 4-inch squares.

In a sauté pan over moderate heat, brown the *cèpes* and ham in the oil.

When the *cèpes* have lost their moisture, add minced garlic. Sauté for only 2 to 3 minutes over a low fire, so as not to burn the garlic. Add the finely chopped parsley and breadcrumbs. Season with salt and pepper.

Spread the squares of meat with the stuffing, roll them up, and tie them with string. Place them on top of a layer of onion, chopped carrots, and the *bouquet garni* in a heavy casserole. Cover and let them sweat—cook without browning—over moderate to low heat.

Then add the white wine, and beef stock.

Bake for 1 hour.

When they are cooked, place your *manchons* on a platter, having removed the strings.

Reduce the remaining sauce and pour it over the *manchons*.

Serves 4.

Game Surprises from Périgueux

6 quail, 6 thrush, or a dozen lark, boned. Save the livers and the bones.
Salt and freshly ground black pepper
1 cup cognac

Filling

3 thick slices bacon, finely chopped
¼ cup fresh bread crumbs
12 button mushrooms, finely chopped
Peelings from 6 sliced truffles [or 1 tablespoon black truffle puree (such as Salsa Tartufata by Urbani, see Sources, page 265), or 1 teaspoon white truffle oil]
6 pieces parchment paper, 15 by 8 inches

Game sauce

Bones from the birds, crushed
1 cup chicken stock
Salt and freshly ground black pepper
¾ cup Madeira

Preheat the oven to 350 degrees.

Place the birds in a bowl and season with salt, pepper, and cognac.

Make the filling by mixing the bacon, bread crumbs, mushrooms, and truffles together in a bowl.

Finely chop the livers of the birds and add to the filling.

Butter some paper as you would when making veal *en papillote* (in a parchment paper parcel). Fold each piece of paper in half, then unfold. Butter both halves of the paper.

Place a heaping tablespoon of filling in the center of the right-hand half. Cover the birds with truffle peelings, puree, or oil. Place a bird on the filling, then top with another heaping tablespoon of filling. Fold the left-hand side of the paper over and fold the edges very tightly to seal in the steam as it cooks. Repeat with the rest of the birds. If using larks, use 2 birds for each package.

Bake the surprise packages on a baking sheet for 25 minutes.

Make a game sauce as follows:

Place the bones in a saucepan with the stock, salt and pepper, and Madeira. Cook over moderate heat and reduce to ¾ cup.

Strain through a fine sieve, pressing down on it well so that you extract all the juices.

Serve the surprises hot. When the guests open their packages, pass the game sauce.

If this dish is cooked slowly and served hot and sufficiently moistened with sauce, it produces complete gustatory satisfaction.

Serves 3 or 6. You must decide whether your guests will eat 1 or 2 packages each.

Hare Sauce from Orignac

This sauce is served with roast hare.

- 2   cups red wine vinegar
- 2   heads garlic, peeled
- 1   hare liver [or 4 chicken livers]
- 1   ½-ounce piece of *beurre manie* (see Glossary,
      page 259) [or 1 tablespoon cornstarch dissolved in
      2 tablespoons cold water]
- 1   tablespoon drippings or olive oil
      Sugar (optional)

Boil the vinegar with the garlic in a sauce pan.

When the garlic is cooked, in about 20 minutes, and the liquid is reduced, add the hare or chicken livers. Boil for a minute until the liver is cooked but still soft enough to crush.

Add the *beurre manie* or dissolved cornstarch, stirring well, to bind the sauce.

Strain the sauce through a sieve, pushing on the garlic and liver to extract every bit of juice. Pour back into the saucepan. Discard the garlic and liver. Add drippings or oil to absorb the acid. The better the drippings, the more delicious the sauce will be. If the sauce still tastes too acidic, add some sugar.

This sauce should have the consistency of a mustard, without any lumps at all.

If you can't stand garlic, remove it when it is cooked, but its perfume is essential to the character and quality of the sauce.

Yield: 2 cups.

Grape Harvester's Turkey Wings

     2   turkey wings, weighing about 3 pounds total
    [1   tablespoon olive oil] or goose fat
     1   onion, finely chopped
     1   carrot, peeled and sliced
     1   *bouquet garni* (see Glossary, page 259)
     1   clove
     1   tablespoon cognac
    1½   cups chicken stock
     6   artichoke hearts, cooked in chicken stock
         [or 6 canned or frozen cooked artichoke hearts,
         cut into thirds]
    1½   pounds red seedless grapes

Preheat the oven to 350 degrees.

Prick the turkey wings with a skewer or toothpick.

Place the oil in a heavy casserole over moderate heat. Brown the turkey wings and then add the chopped onion and carrot, the *bouquet garni*, and the clove. Add the cognac and chicken stock.

Cover and bake for 30 minutes.

Remove the lid and cook for another 15 minutes.

In the meantime, to the cooked artichoke hearts and stock, add the red grapes and heat through for not more than 2 to 3 minutes.

Place the turkey wings on a platter, surrounded with the artichoke hearts and grapes. Strain the turkey juices, reduce if necessary, and pour over the wings.

Serve hot.

Serves 2.

Veal Fanchette

Those who add truffles to this dish are wasters; Fanchette is a serious housewife and not an overindulgent cook.

    2   veal scallops, weighing 6 to 8 ounces each
        Olive oil
        Salt and freshly ground black pepper
    1   cup fresh bread crumbs
    2   shallots, minced
    1   tablespoon parsley, chopped
    2   slices bacon, finely chopped and cooked until crisp
    2   large egg yolks
    1   large egg
    1   tablespoon water
    4   tablespoons unsalted butter

Marinate the veal in the refrigerator from morning to evening or 3 hours in oil, salt and pepper.

Place the bread crumbs on a plate. Add shallots, parsley and bacon bits.

Beat the egg yolks and egg together with the water.

Dip the veal in the beaten eggs, then in the bread crumb mixture.

Sauté 1 veal scallop in the butter over moderate heat until golden, for 2 to 3 minutes each side. Keep it warm as you cook the second scallop.

Serves 2.

Sautéed Chicken Bordelaise

Serve this dish with Potatoes *Pont Neuf*—french fries (see page 81).

    1 3½- to 4-pound chicken with giblets, cut into 9 pieces, (see page 260)
  [6 tablespoons olive oil] or goose fat
    6 shallots, finely sliced
  ⅔ cup chicken stock
    1 tablespoon cognac
    3 cloves garlic, minced
    2 tablespoons parsley, finely chopped
    1 tablespoon olive oil

Heat the oil in a frying pan over moderate heat. Add the chicken pieces and when they are browned, put to the side.

Sauté the shallots until soft.

Add the giblets and cook about 5 minutes.

Spoon off the fat and add the stock and, to be perfect, the cognac. Simmer for 20 minutes or until the chicken is tender.

Before serving, sauté the garlic and parsley with oil in another pan for 2 minutes.

Serve the chicken on a platter, sprinkled with the sautéed garlic and parsley, with french fries around it.

Serve very hot.

Serves 4.

Cèpes *(Porcini)* Bordelaise

Some delicate stomachs may prefer that the garlic is left whole and carefully separated from the *cèpes* after cooking. This is the only thing one can do, for to altogether eliminate the garlic from *Cèpes Bordelaise* would be a monstrous heresy.

1 pound *cèpes* (porcini) [or button mushrooms]
¼ cup olive oil
3 cloves garlic, minced
1 tablespoon parsley, finely chopped

Choose firm small *cèpes* with black caps. Remove the stems and reserve.

Heat 3 tablespoons olive oil in a frying pan over moderate heat. When it is hot, add the mushroom caps and let them brown, then put them in a casserole.

Chop up the mushroom stems. Heat 1 tablespoon olive oil in the frying pan and add the chopped stems, garlic, and parsley. When they are brown, add to the *cèpes* and simmer them covered for 15 minutes over a very low fire.

Serve very hot.

Serves 2 to 3.

Eggplant Bordelaise

¾ cup olive oil
2 pounds medium-size eggplants, cut lengthwise and then across in 1-inch slices
   Salt and freshly ground black pepper
3 cloves garlic, minced
2 tablespoons parsley, finely chopped
2 tablespoons fresh bread crumbs

Heat the oil in a frying pan over moderate to high heat. When it is hot, add the sliced eggplant in batches. Sprinkle with salt and pepper as they cook. When they are golden, put them aside in an oven dish.

Sauté the garlic for 1 to 2 minutes in the same pan, being careful not to burn it. Add the parsley and bread crumbs. Sprinkle this *persillade* mixture over the eggplant before serving.

Serve hot.

Serves 6.

Cassoulet de Castelnaudary

[There are several varieties of *cassoulet* produced in southwest France. This is a very simple version from the town Castelnaudary; Toulouse and Carcassone have their versions also. There are slight differences in the ingredients and the amount of time you are to stir the pot of meat, beans, and bread crumbs!]

    1½   pounds dried white beans
          Cold water
    ½   pound salt pork with rind
          Salt and freshly ground black pepper
    1   clove garlic
    ¾   pound lamb steak taken from the leg or loin chops
    1   pound pork chops
    1   pound small sausages
    1   pound salt pork with rind
    ½   duck or goose, cut in pieces or 8 to 10 pieces of Preserved Duck or Goose (see page 205)
    2   cups fresh bread crumbs

Cook the beans in a large casserole or pot, with water to cover by 4 inches, with pork rind, salt and pepper, and garlic at a simmer for 1 hour or more until just tender.

In the meantime, fry or roast the lamb, pork chops, sausages, and duck until browned.

Add the lamb and pork to the beans, making sure the beans cover the meat. Pour the meat frying juices over. Set aside the sausages and duck.

Cool, cover, and refrigerate overnight.

The next day, bring the *cassoulet* to a simmer on top of the stove. If it is too dry, add some stock or water.

Preheat the oven to 350 degrees.

Add the sausages and preserved duck, if using. Sprinkle the surface with half the bread crumbs and bake for 1 hour, stirring once and covering with the rest of the bread crumbs.

Serve from the casserole.

Serves 8 to 10.

Lombézien *Cake —A Pistachio Charlotte*

This charlotte is even better if it is made the evening before. [The shelled unsalted pistachio nuts needed as an ingredient are found in Indian and health food stores.]

1	recipe vanilla pastry cream (see Glossary, page 262)
½	pound shelled, unsalted pistachio nuts
3	tablespoons unsalted butter, softened, plus more to butter the mold
3	tablespoons sugar
36	sponge fingers, bought
¼	cup heavy cream

Make the vanilla pastry cream. Cool.

Grind the pistachio nuts [in a food processor or blender].

Mix the ground nuts, butter, and sugar together to make a paste and add it to the pastry cream.

Lightly butter a 4-cup charlotte mold (with sloping sides) or soufflé dish before lining it with sponge fingers. Line the mold with the sponge fingers.

Pour the pistachio mixture into the mold and cover with another layer of sponge fingers. Refrigerate it, preferably overnight.

To unmold, run a sharp knife around the edge of the mold. Place a plate over the top of the mold. Turn both over. If the charlotte does not unmold easily, dip it into warm water for 30 seconds and try again.

Whip the cream and pipe a few swirls or rosettes onto the charlotte, especially where the pistachio cream shows through the sponge fingers.

Serves 6 to 8.

Bavarois aux Marrons — *A Chestnut Cream*

[You can use canned, sweetened puree of chestnuts — Bonne Maman is a well-flavored product and comes in a 13-ounce jar. Obviously you will not have to add the sugar and vanilla as in the recipe below.]

40   chestnuts

Caramel syrup
   ½   cup sugar
   ¼   cup water

¾ cup sugar
2 tablespoons water
1 teaspoon vanilla essence
1 packet powdered gelatin, dissolved in ¼ cup
   warm water
½ cup heavy cream, whipped stiff
1 large egg white
   Pinch cream of tartar

Make a small slit in the rounded sides of the chestnuts before cooking them, so you can peel them easily. Cook them in water for 20 minutes, peel them, then [puree in a food processor or] rub them through a food mill.

Make a caramel syrup with ½ cup sugar and ¼ cup water. Melt the sugar in a heavy saucepan over moderate to low heat, and when it is dissolved and the color of straw, carefully add the water. Pour the caramel into a charlotte mold and swirl it around to cover the bottom and sides.

Melt ¾ cup sugar with 2 tablespoons water. Add this syrup and the vanilla to the pureed chestnuts.

Stir the gelatin briskly into the puree.

Whip the cream until stiff and add to the chestnut puree, folding in well. Beat egg whites until stiff and fold in. Pour the mixture into the mold. Refrigerate or freeze—your choice.

To unmold, place a plate over the top of the mold. Turn both over. If the cream does not come out easily, dip the mold into warm water for 30 seconds and try again.

Serves 6 to 8.

Coffee, Tea, and Healthful Drinks

Coffee

In order to make good coffee, according to an old family tradition, you have to grind it in a coffee mill. This principle alone has given rise to much discussion: some say that the surface of the mill should be flat, others say it should be rounded.

In truth, in order to make good coffee, you must start with good coffee beans. The best is a mixture of a third mocha, a third Bourbon, and a third Martinique.

According to the number of cups you want to prepare, fill the mill more or less with 20 grams (2 tablespoons) per cup. It's important that the coffee be finely ground, in order to give the water a strong flavor.

When you have ground the coffee, place it in the top of the *cafetière* [drip coffee pot] so that it makes a column about eight centimeters (3 inches) high. Pour some very hot water over it to pack it down, then pour small quantities of boiling water on top so that it filters through the small holes of the *cafetière*. Keep the coffee warm in a *bain-marie* (see Glossary, page 259).

Tea

Tea must be made with *boiling*, not hot, water. Preheat the teapot with very hot water before putting the tea in it.

Place about a coffeespoon of tea per cup into the teapot.

Pour boiling water over the tea leaves, stir with a spoon, cover, and leave to infuse for 2 minutes. Serve.

Tea that has infused for too long takes on a bitter taste that is detestable.

Chamomile

To make a good chamomile drink you have to have picked the flowers in a country garden and dried them. It is also necessary to be careful not to use too many flowers. Three sprigs is enough for 4 cups. Otherwise the drink becomes bitter and loses all its virtue. Steep the flowers in boiling water.

A quarter teaspoon of orange-flower water [available from health food stores and pharmacies] added to each cup gives it a delicious taste.

Hot Lemonade

Use 1 slice of lemon and 2 teaspoons sugar for each cup.

Pour on boiling water, stir well, and drink hot.

This is excellent for the digestion.

Poule (Chicken) Milk

Sweet chicken milk is made as follows:

     1   large egg yolk
     3   tablespoons sugar
     1   cup boiling water
     ¼   teaspoon orange-flower water

Place the egg yolk in a bowl. Blend in the sugar. Add boiling water to which you have added orange-flower water.

Take the chicken milk to the bedroom of a child with a cold. It will make his cold better, and it will amuse him to drink it.

Afterword

Pampille, born Marthe Allard in 1878, is not herself famous, but she married a man who became very well known: Leon Daudet, the son of Alphonse Daudet the poet. Leon became famous for his writings on politics and related subjects.

Pampille, in her own right, has left a legacy of four books and some articles in *L'Action Française*. The *Contes des Deux Mères/Stories from Two Mothers* (1914) are stories for children, and another book called *Comment Devenir Bonne Maîtresse de la Maison/How to Become a Good Mistress of the House* was published in 1951. Nineteen-hundred-and-twenty-six saw the appearance of her book *La Vie et La Mort de Philippe*. This is a heart-rending memoir of her son, who died at the age of fourteen. He was found shot in the head in a Paris taxi, presumably assassinated because of his royalist parents.

Marthe was given her writing name *Pampille* by a friend named Lemaître. She was fine featured and beautiful. Leon was a gourmand, a large man, a hearty eater and drinker. A quote from Leon in a biography by Paul Clebert describes them as ". . . she, light as a butterfly, me behind round as a melon."

She was a model mother, housekeeper, and hostess, and was known to be calm, cultivated, and energetic. She was a political reactionary who helped persuade Leon to become a royalist, and was one of the first to join *La Ligue de la Patrie*, a royalist group. Her strong, intelligent, religious character stood her in good stead with Leon. She obviously enjoyed being a wife and mother and they had a happy and fulfilled marriage, marred only by the death of Philippe, one of their three children.

Leon and Marthe, who were cousins, met in Touraine, where Leon's mother and father, Alphonse and Julia Daudet, stayed when not in Provence. Leon and Pampille loved to visit Normandy, Brittany, and other regions of France, but they lived for the most part in Paris, staying through the bombardments in the First World War. Leon was a connoisseur of wine, as his red face attested. The couple's consuming interest in food made them very particular in their likes and dislikes — they sent for butter and wine from Touraine, for instance.

In an article in *L'Action Française*, Leon decried the lack of fresh bread on Mondays and urged the bakeries to stay open every day. He associated good health with food and he recommended an infallible cure to combat *la grippe* (flu). He instructed the sick person to "stay in bed in a warm room for five days, eating on the first day *Bouillabaisse*, accompanied with Château Neuf; *Bourride* the second day, and garlic soup for dinner. On the third day a *pot-au-feu* with Beaujolais, Bourgueil or Bordeaux; on the fourth day, if you are not cured, eat a lamb cutlet at lunch with a red Bordeaux and if you are better, eat two. In the evening, drink an entire bottle of Champagne. Don't get up until the fifth day. . . ."

And he loved garlic . . . " *L'aioli*, a garlic-flavored mayonnaise, is a sure method of escaping illness or death. Even though it might kill your friends, the absence of *aioli* can kill." Pampille was more reserved about garlic.

Leon died in 1942 in his beloved Provence, at St. Remy. Pampille died in 1960.

Pampille — Biographical notes

1878   Born Marthe Allard in Champrosay, 27 kms southeast of Paris.

1902   Aged 24, met her cousin Leon Daudet in Touraine, where his family had a second home. The Allard family home was also there.

1903   Became Leon Daudet's second wife. Honeymoon in Madrid, Gibraltar, and Provence. Lived in Paris in Bourg-la-Reine on the southern outskirts.

1906   On their third anniversary they went to Normandy, St. Nazaire, Le Croisic, Guérande, and Piriac.

1908   Leon founded *L'Action Française* with Charles Maurras.

1909   Philippe Daudet born.

1914   Marthe wrote *Les Contes des Deux Mères*, with Mme de Bussac (book in the *Bibliothèque Nationale*). She also wrote an article in *L'Action Française*: "Comment Elever Nos Filles," and many small paragraphs about cooking.

1915   François Daudet born.

1918   Clare Daudet born. Pampille had a difficult time giving birth and was afraid of dying. The family took refuge in Normandy because of the bombardment of Paris.

1919   *Les Bons Plats de France* published. 1920 and 1921 Marcel Proust mentions Pampille in volumes II and III of *Remembrance of Things Past*.

1923   Philippe was missing for five days. Pampille thought he had committed suicide, but found a small notification in *Le Petit Parisien* of a young man who had been found dead in a taxi with a head wound. Was it an assassination because his father was a royalist?

1926   Pampille publishes *La Vie et La Mort de Philippe*
1942   Leon Daudet dies in Provence—St. Remy.
1951   Pampille publishes *Comme Devenir Bonne Maîtresse du Maison*
1960   Pampille dies, also Leon Daudet's son Charles by first marriage.
1969   Clare Daudet dies.
1970   François Daudet dies.

Glossary

Bain-marie — A *bain-marie* is used to keep food warm and prevent further cooking. Place the food in its container into a larger container (the *bain-marie*) half filled with hot water. Custards, soufflés, and other delicate dishes that are baked are placed, in their dishes or molds, in a baking pan filled halfway with hot water.

Beurre manie — *Beurre manie* is added to sauces to thicken them at the end of cooking. Mix equal parts of butter and flour together: 4 tablespoons flour to the same amount of soft butter is a useful amount. Work the two together and then form 4 balls with your fingers or a spoon. Wrap the balls separately in plastic wrap and store in the refrigerator.

Blood — Blood was often used to thicken sauces that accompany the animal itself. As an alternate thickener, use fine bread crumbs, finely ground almonds, or even the crushed liver of the animal. Of course these additions will not produce a smooth sauce. If this is important to you, use cornstarch, potato flour, or *beurre manie* (see above) instead.

Bouillie — *Bouillie* is a thick gruel made by cooking flour, bread, or bread crumbs with milk or water.

Bouquet garni — A *bouquet garni* consists of a few sprigs of parsley, fresh thyme, a bay leaf, and, when desired, a smashed clove of garlic. It is perhaps wiser to include only parsley stems, as the leaves may come off during cooking and spoil the look of a totally white sauce, as in Chicken Fricassee (see page 140). Tie the herbs together with string (fold them over on themselves if they are long) or tie in cheesecloth. Always remove the bundle before serving. If straining at the end of cooking, just throw the herbs in without tying them. You may find that you can buy already assembled *bouquet garni*—dried herbs wrapped in cheesecloth bundles.

Chicken, how to cut into nine pieces before cooking—This is called *selon les regles* in French. First carve off the legs (that includes the thigh and drumstick) in one piece. Cut and separate the thighs from the drumstick. Cut the whole breast away from the back and divide it in two down the center of the breast bone. Cut across each breast with a diagonal cut. You now have eight pieces and the back is the ninth piece. As a refinement you can cut the two breasts off the breast bone, so they are boneless.

Chipolatas —Chipolatas are small pork sausages or frankfurter-type sausages, 2 to 4 inches long; they can be used as cocktail sausages.

Court-bouillon — *Court-bouillon* is a flavored liquid used for poaching meat, fish, or chicken. There must be enough liquid to cover the item. A *court-bouillon* may include any of the following: water, white wine, or stock flavored with onion, carrot, garlic, a *bouquet garni* (see above), parsley stalks, thyme, chervil, bay leaf, tarragon, cayenne, cloves, and salt and pepper. The *court-bouillon* should be cooked alone for 20 to 30 minutes so that the liquid is thoroughly flavored before adding the item to be poached.

Crème fraîche — *Crème fraîche* is a thick cream with a little kick to it—a slightly sour taste. It is not unlike sour cream, which can be substituted if necessary. You can buy *crème fraîche* in well-stocked stores (it comes in 10-ounce containers) or you can make your own, which may turn out to be a little thinner.

Ingredients

1   cup heavy cream
¼   cup buttermilk

Place the ingredients in a bowl and stir to combine. Place the bowl, covered, in a warm place (70 degrees) for about 8 hours or until the cream sets and thickens. Refrigerate for up to 10 days.

Egg-yolk glaze—Egg-yolk glaze gives a nice sheen and golden color to pastries. Mix 1 large egg yolk with 1 tablespoon water. Use a pastry brush to glaze.

Fines herbes—This delightful mixture of herbs is used in many French dishes, from omelets to salads. Chop 1 or 2 tablespoons each fresh parsley, chervil, chives, and tarragon. If you cannot find chervil, which is a pretty herb that looks a little like parsley and tastes slightly of anise, use a little more tarragon.

Fritonnière—As far as I can make out, a *fritonnière* is a large infuser—a fine mesh container that can be filled with a highly flavored item, such as ham, dunked into a stock or soup to flavor, and then removed before serving. *Fritons* are small fatty bits of pork.

Gelatin leaves—Gelatin is available in leaf and, more commonly, powdered form. Seven leaves are the equivalent to 1 envelope of powdered gelatin.

Hermetically seal, how to—In order to hermetically seal a saucepan, use parchment paper, aluminum foil, and a close-fitting lid.

Lard, how to—Larding was necessary when meat was very lean and tough and added fat was needed to moisten and flavor it. Long, ¼- to ½-inch-wide threads of pork fat (lardons) were sewn with larding needles into the meat at intervals of 1 to 2 inches.

Marmite—A *marmite* is a large 8-quart capacity stockpot about 12 inches in diameter and 15 inches high. Any pot that works will do.

Mussels, how to clean—Clean mussels by soaking them in a sink of cold water and rubbing them together so that any barnacles or sand sticking to them falls off. Brush them with a scourer or scrape them with a knife, if necessary. Pull off the "beards" (the byssal threads that stick out of the join of the shells) only 20 minutes before cooking. Removing the mussels' beards starts their death throes, and you want to cook only live mussels.

Pastry cream—
    2   cups milk
    1   vanilla bean, split, or 1 teaspoon vanilla extract
    6   large egg yolks
    ½   cup sugar
    3   tablespoons all-purpose flour, or 1 tablespoon
        all-purpose flour and 2 tablespoons cornstarch.

Bring the milk and vanilla bean to a simmer. Remove from the fire and leave to infuse for 10 minutes.

Whisk together the egg yolks and sugar until thick—about 2 minutes. Whisk in the flour.

Strain the milk into the egg-yolk mixture, reserving the vanilla bean to use again. Place in a saucepan over a moderate fire and whisk until the mixture thickens. Cook for 2 more minutes, whisking all the time, then pour into a bowl—if using vanilla extract, add it now.

Pâté brisée—Variations I and II
I. For Tarte au Fromage Blanc *(see page 162)*
    and Onion Tart (see page 161)

　　1¼　cups all-purpose flour
　　　　Pinch salt
　　　4　ounces unsalted butter
3 to 4　tablespoons ice water

II. For Quiche Lorraine (see page 168)
　　1¼　cups all-purpose flour
　　　　Pinch salt
　　　3　ounces unsalted butter
3 to 4　tablespoons ice water.

Combine the flour, salt, and butter with your fingers or a pastry cutter until the mixture resembles breadcrumbs. This can also be done in the food processor. Add enough water to form a dough. Flatten the pastry into a disc about ½ inch thick. Wrap in plastic wrap and chill for 40 minutes.

Pearl onions, how to peel — Trim off the bottom root end only. Bring a pot of water to a boil. When you have finished trimming all the onions, throw them in the boiling water. Lower the heat and cook for 5 minutes. Drain and cool with cold water. Peel the skins off the onions.

Pot-au-feu — A *pot-au-feu* is a version of a *marmite*, or stockpot. Its capacity should be at least 8 quarts.

Quatre épices (Four spices) —
Mix together: 3 teaspoons ground black pepper, 1 teaspoon nutmeg, 1 teaspoon cinnamon, and ¼ teaspoon ground cloves. Store in a jar.

Sometimes allspice, also known as *quatre épices* in France, is used instead of the above mixture.

Roux — A *roux* is used to thicken a sauce.
Melt butter or fat in a pan over moderate heat and sprinkle flour over. Stir well. Cook over a low fire until the mixture colors a little — about 2 minutes. Add hot or cold liquid and stir

again, using a whisk, until the mixture comes to a boil and thickens. Cook another 2 to 5 minutes to rid the sauce of any floury taste. The specific amounts of butter, flour, and liquid are indicated in particular recipes.

Truffles — Truffles are impossibly high in price nowadays. Those that can should afford the expense but for others it is a good idea to find a product called *Salsa Tartufata*, made by Urbani. It is a black truffle puree made of truffles, mushrooms, and olive oil. It is sold in 1-ounce jars in specialty stores for about $8. You can also buy *white truffle oil*, which has a strong aroma of truffles and must be used sparingly. See Sources, page 265.

Verjus — *Verjus* is the first pressing of green or unripe grapes. It is raw and unfermented and can be preserved with a little salt. You may use vinegar diluted with a little water.

Vine shoots — Vine shoots or cuttings are now burned in outdoor grills to give extra flavor to food.

Sources

Duck Liver

D'Artagnan
399-419 St. Paul Ave.
Jersey City, NJ 07306
(800) 327-8246

Hudson Valley Foiegras
RR #1, Box 69
Ferndale, NY 12734
(914) 292-2500

Country Ham

W.G. White Company
642 North Cherry St.
Winston-Salem, NC 27101
(910) 723-1669

The Smithfield Collection
401 North Church St.
Smithfield, VA 23430
(800) 628-2242

S. Wallace Edwards & Sons
P.O. Box 25
Surry, VA 23883
(800) 222-4267

Pepper Melange

Select Origins
P.O. Box 1748
Mansfield, OH 44901
(800) 965-9979
(419) 522-2722

Crawfish
(available from early
November through July)

Randol's
2350 Kaliste Saloom Rd.
Lafayette, LA 70508
(800) 962-2586

Frog Legs and Crawfish

Bayou Land Seafood
1008 Vincent Berard Rd.
Breaux Bridge, LA 70517
(318) 667-7407

Urbani Truffles
and Salsa Tartufata

Urbani USA Wholesale
    Division
29-24 40th Ave.
Long Island City, NY 11101
(718) 392-5050

Shelled Black Walnuts

Missouri Dandy Pantry
212 Hammons Dr. East
Stockton, MO 65785
(800) 872-6879

American Spoon Foods
411 East Lake St.
Petoskey, MI 49770
(616) 347-9030

Sunnyland Farms, Inc.
Rte. 1
Albany, GA 31703
(912) 883-3085

William F. Weber
8237 Ridgefield Rd.
Pensacola, FL 32514
(904) 476-4908

Equivalent Measures

Liquid and Dry Measure Equivalencies

CUSTOMARY		METRIC	
¼	teaspoon	1.25	milliliters
½	teaspoon	2.5	milliliters
1	teaspoon	5	milliliters
1	tablespoon	15	milliliters
1	fluid ounce	30	milliliters
¼	cup	60	milliliters
⅓	cup	80	milliliters
½	cup	120	milliliters
1	cup	240	milliliters
1	pint (2 cups)	480	milliliters
1	quart (4 cups, 32 ounces)	960	milliters (.96 liters)
1	gallon (4 quarts)	3.84	liters
1	ounce (by weight)	28	grams
¼	pound (4 ounces)	114	grams
1	pound (16 ounces)	454	grams
2.2	pounds	1	kilogram (1000 grams)

Oven Temperature Equivalencies

DESCRIPTION	FAHRENHEIT	CELSIUS
Cool	200	90
Very slow	250	120
Slow	300–325	150–160
Moderately slow	325–350	160–180
Moderate	350–375	180–190
Moderately hot	375–400	190–200
Hot	400–450	200–230
Very hot	450–500	230–260

Index of Recipes